BOTTLE

BOTTLE

The Completely True Story of an Ex-Football Hooligan

Steve Fist with Ivor Baddiel

MAINSTREAM
PUBLISHING

EDINBURGH AND LONDON

First published in Great Britain in 2005 by
MAINSTREAM PUBLISHING COMPANY
(EDINBURGH) LTD
7 Albany Street
Edinburgh EH1 3UG

ISBN 1 84018 973 8

A catalogue record for this book is available
from the British Library

Typeset in Baskerville Book and MMCutout

Printed in Great Britain by
Cox & Wyman Ltd

intro=fucking=duction

If there's one thing that my years as a football hooligan taught me, it's this: West Ham are cunts; Arsenal are cunts; Spurs are fucking cunts. They're all cunts, the lot of them, and they fucking deserve what's coming to them. What's more, you're a cunt. Yes, you, reading this, you're a cunt and 20 years ago I'd've fucking mullahed you. Fucking kicked your fucking head in, and then fucking kicked it in some more. Got it? I might still fucking do it now if you had it coming to you, but, like, there's the rub. Might. Might, might, might, might, might. I mean, that's no fucking good is it? 'You might get your fucking head kicked in.' What sort of chant is that? 'You might be going home in a London ambulance.' Naw, fuck that, 25 years ago you *were* fucking going home in a London ambulance mate, no fucking doubt about it, end of. Now, now it's might. Which is still something, right. You can't start taking the fucking piss, right. Don't expect to fucking make me look like a mug cause then it won't be might any more it'll be back to fucking, right, here's what's fucking coming to you. But when you get to my age, when you've kicked the living shit out of as many people as I have, when you've glassed as many cunts as I have, well, you want to pass it on don't you? It's like your civic hooligan duty isn't it? Naw, course it fucking ain't. The truth is there's all these other cunts out there who used to kick the shit out of people week in week out, and now they're all making fucking dosh writing about it, which is making me look like a fucking mug, AND NO ONE MAKES ME LOOK LIKE A MUG. So I'm going to fucking do it, right? Simple. But this is no fucking apology for a misspent youth. This is no socio-fucking-logical the-fucking-sis. This is a fucking manual. Yeah. Cause I know it all. All the fucking tricks of the trade. How to send the Old Bill on a fucking wild-goose chase so you can sort it out to go off where you want it to go off. How two of you – top boys, mind – can empty a fucking boozer full of cunts and send them running down the road with their tails between their legs. How to set up and run your own firm. Loadsa stuff. Solid gold. It's all in here. So fucking read on if you don't want to be made to look like a mug, and remember, if there's one lesson my years as a hooligan fucking taught me, it's this: don't run from not no one, not so not never, right?

chapter fucking one

The idea for this book came to me the other day when I was down The Pissflaps and Labia having a drink with three top lads from the old Millwall firm the BYC, Bastard Young Cannibals. They're a real firm now, of accountants; we still meet up from time to time to yak about the old days and do my tax returns. Anyway, after we'd kicked the absolute living shit out of each other, Twatter Dave, a thickset geezer who was fucking thick as well, turned to me, blood pouring out of a deep gash I'd inflicted on his forehead, and said, 'You know, Coconut' – one of my many nicknames from back then, based on the fact that more likely than not I was going to smash yer fucking head open like one and watch yer fucking brains drain out like milk if you didn't fucking watch it;

Bill the Face thought it up, I kind of liked it – "Ow many times must we 'ave kicked the shit out of each other?' I belted him one and said, 'I don't fucking know, but that's one more.' The two other cunts laughed, so I twatted them again and then it all went off and we ended up being chased by fucking plod down the Old Kent Road (Old Bill Road, more like, the way they just seem to turn up there as soon as it goes off).

Anyway, once I'd ducked down a side alley and lost the cunts, I did get to thinking about what Twatter had said. And not just him and the other Millwall boys, but the whole fucking lot. How many broken noses must there have been? How many cracked and bruised ribs? How many punctured lungs and near-fatalities? (How many fatalities for that matter?) I mean, I thought, what was the point if it was all just going to be forgotten like some fucking meaningless pile of shit? So that's when I decided, right there, amongst the rotting vegetables, empty fucking McDonald's cartons, rancid spunk-filled old condoms and decaying spunk-filled old sewing machines, that my life wasn't going to be thrown away like the very shite I was hiding in. I was going to do something about it. Write the fucker down.

It gave me a good feeling all over deciding that, the sort of feeling I used to get when I was chasing three Leeds cunts down the Fulham Road knowing that when I caught one of them, very soon, his face was going to resemble fucking muesli and that's all he'd be eating for a long time after an' all. Standing up, I felt so good I fucking head-butted a lamp-post for looking at me.

When I got home, after having a shit, I just started to write. It was all fucking there, every fucking moment, apart from the ones I couldn't remember. Cause you don't forget stuff like that, you don't forget the fucking life I've had, unless you're a fucking headcase or a schizo or an amnesiac or something. So here it is, the whole fucking lot.

chapter fucking two

My old man first took me to football in 1969, when I was five. I remember it like it was the day before yesterday. We'd just been to the tattoo shop. He was having a fly put onto the spider's web tattoo that covered his face and I was having H-A-T-E put on my left hand. I'd had L-O-V-E done the week before and would've had H-A-T-E done at the same time but the old cunt had a fucking run-in with some geezer in the shop, so we had to leg it. It meant spending a week at fucking nursery with L-O-V-E on my right hand and nothing on my left. The other kids had a fucking field day. Slaughtered me for it. I don't think I've ever really forgiven him for that. So we'd left the shop and were walking back home when I said, 'Nutter' – Nutter Bill, as my Dad was called round our way; he liked me to call him that, said if I was to be a real man that's what I had to call him, 'Daddy' and 'Dad', that was for poofs, he said – 'where are all these people going?'

'Fuck me,' the old tosser said, looking around. 'There must be fucking football on today.'

'Oi, mate,' he said to some geezer walking next to him, 'is there fucking football on today or fucking what?'

'I, er, honestly, I don't want any trouble, please, I'm just, I just want to get a paper,' said the geezer.

'You fucking what?' said Nutter. 'You taking the fucking piss, mate?'

Well, the geezer had it coming to him, right, fucking wanker. So after me old man had given him the proverbial Dollis Hill snog – cause that was our manor, Dollis Hill – broke his nose in eight places, we found out that there was football on that day, and it was only fucking Everton coming to town, wasn't it? Fucking Scousers.

Even at that age I hated Scousers. Fucking thieving scumbags, the lot of them. There was one at my nursery, ugly-looking runt, said his old man couldn't get a fucking job up there so he'd come down looking for work. Yeah, looking to fucking leech off the likes of us decent folk more like. Course, I didn't know then that Everton were Scousers.

''Ere, Nutter,' I said, looking up at the old boy, my eyes agog, full to the brim of childhood innocence, 'what the fuck are Everton?'

'Not "what", son,' he said, '"who". Everton are the worst fucking cunts imaginable.'

'Not fucking Geordies,' I said as if the very breath within my lungs had been sucked out with the force of a hurricane, tornado and gale together.

'Naw, son, naw, they ain't fucking Geordies. They're worse than that. Everton are fucking Scousers.'

And the way he said it, I knew he wasn't joking. Cause he did like to joke, specially about Scousers. He once told me the neighbour's new dog was a Scouser. Only went and fucking poisoned it, didn't I? Geezer next door nearly fucking throttled me. I don't think I've ever really forgiven him for that. The old man, I mean, not the geezer next door; I got *him* back by poisoning him as well. He spent a week in intensive. Never grassed me up mind. Well, it was only a laugh anyway. Naw, when my old fella said that, he meant it. He had that look in his eye, the same look he used to get just before lamping the old girl: kind of chilling, but excited and strangely sensitive at the same time. Cause he loved it, didn't he, hurting people, it was the closest he ever came to expressing emotion.

As for me, my five-year-old blood was boiling.

'Scousers,' I thought. 'Fucking Scousers. Fucking, fucking Scousers. Fucking, fucking, fucking Scousers. Fucking, fucking, fucking, fucking Scousers.'

So now we knew what was going on, we were like a team with a mission. Nutter was smoking fag after fag, thinking about what we were going to do. He was

13

charged, it was electrifying. In that moment I looked up at him and saw him like never before. It was like I was seeing the real him for the very first time and all the other hims that I'd seen before were not really him, more quasi, neo, faux hims, if you like (all cunts, mind). Every sinew of his body was taut. His chest puffed out like a hot-air balloon, he was drenched in sweat, so much so that droplets of thick, gooey perspiration monsooned down upon me.

'They're near, son,' he said, sniffing the air. 'Come on.'

As usual in situations like this, his sense of smell went into overdrive.

And then we were off. Running like two startled gazelles. I didn't know where we were going or what we were doing, but I was flying. Nutter started lashing out mindlessly at anyone who got in our way, shouting and screaming 'Scouser cunts' as he did so. I leapt over body after body as they fell crashing to the ground, their Scousers' faces contorted in agony.

'And this is from me, ya Scouse cunt,' I said as I jumped on their faces with my junior Doc Martenettes – four-hole, plasticine toecapped.

After what seemed like five minutes but was probably nearer four, we arrived at the stadium. Stamford Bridge. Home of Chelsea Football Club and my second home for the next 25 years. Course, I didn't know that then. All I knew then was that this thing called football was on and that fucking Scouse cunts Everton were in town. To be honest, looking back, I don't think at the time I even connected the two, football and Everton. It was like Everton were Daleks from *Doctor Who* and football was Klingons from *Star Trek*: sort of the same, but also totally fucking unconnected. How could they come together? OK, they were on the same channel sometimes, but they never appeared in each other's shows, did they? No, in my five-year-old mind, the only thing waiting for us in that colossus of a stadium was more Scousers. I thought the cunts had been rounded up by the likes of my dad and were waiting for us to come in and give them a good kicking.

Once inside, though, after the old man had tucked me under his jacket and clambered over a wall – he never paid for nothing if he could help it, said he wasn't going to waste what money he had by spending it – I realised that there was more. My young mind was awakened to football. It was like I'd suddenly realised that in the Venn diagram, football was the biggest circle and all the other stuff was smaller circles inside. Or, if you like, in the pie chart, football was the pie and Everton, Chelsea, the Old Bill, the Shed, the North Bank, the programme sellers, the hot dogs, even the fucking pies themselves (not the one in the pie chart, the ones they were selling at the match), everything else was just pieces of the pie. It was a fucking magical moment, like Einstein discovering the theory of relativity except a million times more exciting cause along with all the other stuff, there was still fucking Scousers to shit on. It was about as much as my little mind could take. If I'd been older, I would have come in my pants.

'Look over there, son,' Nutter said, using the leg he'd ripped off the bloke next to him to point to a small section of the crowd surrounded by Old Bill. He took the responsibility of my hooligan upbringing very seriously and having sensed that I'd drifted, he was keen to get me back to the job in hand.

I focused in on the small group of travelling Evertonians, my ever-developing sense of hatred and bigotry in full flow. They'd not come down particularly heavy-handed that day, but the few of them that were there were taking the fucking living piss. Right in front of our fucking noses, in our very own back yard, they'd laid out a small rug and were enjoying a light picnic of various nibbles and Chardonnay. If nothing else, that marked them out as cunts. But if they'd thought they were here for a bit of a fucking jolly, they were very fucking wrong. Similarly, if they'd thought they were here for a bit of having the piss taken out of them and some gentle tongue-lashing, they weren't so wrong, but not that right. Likewise, if they thought they were here to have their bollocks pulled off and fed to dogs, they were right, metaphorically, though not in actuality. But, if they thought they were here to receive a damn good hiding at the hands of the top Chelsea firm, then they should have given themselves a pat on the back, cause they'd got it right. But I wasn't telepathic so I had no fucking idea what they were thinking.

As the players ran out and the game started, Nutter made sure I wasn't distracted by the goings-on on the pitch. He led me through a throng of what I later discovered were 'fans', a strange breed of attendee not, apparently, there for the rucking at all. To this day, I've always found the notion of fans a little odd, but for the most part they were a minority and didn't spoil things for the rest of us.

We alighted right next to the thin blue line surrounding the Everton boys. Nutter hated the police. I think it was because when they nicked him one time for drunk and disorderly, he was anally raped by a whole constabulary. Or perhaps it was because when he was a little boy, he was given a policeman's hat one Christmas and the dog pissed in it. Then again, it could have been a genetic predisposition. Either way, he hated the cunts, and now he was faced with about two ton of the bastards between him and the Scousers. (That's two hundred coppers, not two tonnes' worth of coppers in weight, though funnily enough the combined weight of two hundred coppers might be two tonnes.)

A mere mortal might have baulked in this situation, but not my old boy, no cunting way. Nothing was going to stop him having his fun.

Over the other side of the Everton lot, we saw another Chelsea firm gathering. This always pissed Nutter off cause he wasn't part of a firm himself, he *was* a firm. That's right, a firm of one, and the most feared firm of them all. He called his firm Nutter's Firm after himself and ran it like an army. If he ever stepped out of line he was well fucking hard on himself. He once decided to ambush a Manchester United firm who were drinking in The Bastard and Paedophile on the King's Road, only to get so pissed himself that he forgot where he was going to fucking ambush them. He gave himself a right good kicking after that. Fucking wanker.

But today's job was going to go like a well-oiled and well-greased machine, so when he saw the other Chelsea firm getting ready to have a go, he was having none of it. Without so much as a by your leave he walked straight through the coppers, straight through the Evertonians and up to the other firm.

'Oi,' he said to their top boy, a severely disabled geezer in a wheelchair.

'Yeah?' said their top boy through his voice box.

'Yeah?' said Nutter.

'Yeah?' came the reply.

'Yeah?' said Nutter.

'Yeah?'

'Yeah?'

'Yeah?'

This went on for about ten minutes or so, after which they both said, 'Come on, then,' to each other for fifteen minutes and then, 'Do you fucking want some?' for another five. I tell you, it was an education. It was like watching one of them fucking nature programmes on the telly. There they were. Two fully-grown bull walruses ready to have it out to see who would be the dominant male in the pack. Course, that wouldn't then mean that whoever won could go round impregnating every female in the pack when they were on heat, though to be fair, that's pretty much what Nutter did anyway. No. It was about pride, face, front, gall, temerity, barefaced cheek, nerve, chutzpah. Yeah, whoever came out on top would strut all right.

Finally, it kicked off. Nutter threw the quadriplege onto the pitch and kicked his teeth in whilst the Chelsea goalkeeper, Peter 'The Cat' Bonetti, jumped on his back and tried to bite his ear off. It was all over in about 30 seconds, but it had been well worth it.

Walking home after the game that day, I felt I'd really bonded with me dad. He wasn't a man of many words, he preferred to mime things, but through his actions, he'd opened a door in my mind, shone a light into it and said, 'There, have some of that, you cunt.'

It was a seminal moment for me, more so because I never saw him again after that. On the way home, some bloke looked at him a bit funny and he run the cunt. I know Nutter caught the geezer cause I heard the screams, but waiting there in the middle of that busy roundabout, somehow I knew he wasn't coming back.

Three weeks later, after a nationwide appeal and a massive search, I was found, scavenging for scraps round the back of a butcher's in Burnley. When I got home, my mum told me that Nutter hadn't returned. I still remember her exact words.

'The cunt's fucked off. Let's hope he don't come back. Good fucking riddance. Now where are me fucking fags?'

Twenty years later during a ruck outside Villa Park, I had a set to with a guy who looked exactly like Nutter. He had a spider's web tattoo on his face and his mates were calling him Nutter. His smell brought back very early memories. He had a scar shaped like Dr Fox underneath his left thumbnail just like Nutter had. And he showed me his birth certificate, his passport and his driving licence. But I couldn't be sure. I couldn't be sure.

chapter fucking three

After years of badgering my mum and attacking her with various sharp implements, she finally let me go to football on my own when I was ten. Chelsea versus Slovan Bratislava in the UEFA Cup. It used to be the Fairs Cup, why the fuckers changed it I'll never fucking know, it'll always be the Fairs Cup to me.

Truth be told, my mum didn't exactly agree to me going. When she wasn't looking, I slipped some Valium into her vodka (we didn't have Rohypnol back then, more's the pity) and when she was double comatose, I went up to her and asked if I could go to the game. She never said no, didn't say anything, in fact, so I took that as a yes. She was still fucking comatose when I snuck back in at midnight and when I woke up the following morning, which made me think I'd used too much Valium, but it's better to be sure, eh?

I met up with me mates Gal, Gal, Gal and Steve round the back of the chippy. Gal was a bit down, like, cause he'd done the same as me with the Valium only, being the fucking muppet he was, he'd only overdone it and fucking killed his ma, hadn't he?

'Gal, mate,' I said, sensing that if I didn't think of something to say soon he'd leg it back to his house leaving us short-handed, 'Gal, she was gonna fucking die one day, weren't she? You done yourself a favour by finishing her off now. No fucking waiting around for when it's gonna happen. And now there ain't no one around to tell you you can't fucking go to football, right? So you should be fucking flying, mate. On cloud fucking nine.'

See, even then, I had the gift of the fucking gab. I could sell shit to a coprophile, me. Anyway, it worked. Gal saw my point of view. Well, he couldn't very well not after I went on to tell him that he could either come with us or have the living wank kicked out of him.

So we set off, me and me crew, me firm, me boys. Little did we know then that we were taking the first steps on a journey that would last 25 years and see us rucking in every fucking continent of the world. No. We just thought we was going to football, going to give the Bratislavan cunts a hiding, teach them not to fucking come over here lording it up with their fucking poncy East-European ways.

We met up with Steve, Gal, Steve and Gal in The Jism and Jockstrap about 7.15. It was no hassle getting into the boozer, everyone knew I was Nutter's boy and that counted for something round Chelsea. A couple of times some unknowing geezers tried it on, tried to say that we was too fucking young to be out boozing and should fuck off home to our mams, Gal excluded obviously. Well, they were put bang to rights, I can tell you.

'Oi, that's Nutter's boy,' someone would say, 'Leave it if you know what's good for you.'

And they did.

So there we were in The Jism and Jockstrap.

''Ere,' said Steve.

'What?' said Gal.

'Steve reckons there's a Bratislavan firm on their way down from the station. He says they ain't come too heavy-handed. Reckons they're up for it an' all.'

Well, that was just what we all wanted to hear. We finished our Kahluas and headed off to meet the fucking Slovan bastards.

Outside the pub, there was an eerie silence, the kind of silence that said only one thing, silently. Trouble.

'Gal,' I said.

'Yeah?' said Gal.

'You, Gal and Steve go round the back of the bookies and wait there. We'll run 'em in that direction. When you hear them coming, you know what to do.'

'No,' said Gal.

'You do,' I said.

'No, honestly, I don't,' said Gal.

'You fucking jump out and give them the biggest fucking kicking of their fucking lives, all right?' I said.

'Oh,' said Gal. 'Right.'

So they set off, leaving us lying in wait down the side of the pub. It wasn't long before we heard the Bratislavan roar go up.

'Szcyzsy zxszsyt gyggyzst rystsyzzkls fucking heads kicked in!'

Well, that was like a red rag to a bull, a carrot to a donkey and something magnetic to a magnet. We fucking legged it from down the side of the pub and ran out into the centre of the road to meet the Czech wankers. That was when we realised that what Steve had told Gal about what Steve had said about them not having come heavy-handed was fucking on the money. To be exact, there was all of one of them. If that isn't not coming heavy-handed I don't know what is not coming heavy-handed.

But as far as I was concerned, one was one too many. He was going to get what was coming to him and it wasn't a fucking blintz or whatever shite it was that passed for food over there. But there was a problem. The Bratislavan cunt might not have come to our manor mob-handed, but the fucking Old Bill had. This one cunt all dressed up in his Slovakian bovver boots, dinner jacket and bow tie only had fucking 500 Old Bill escorting him to the ground.

'Gal,' I said.

'Yeah?' he said.

'I want you, Gal, Gal and Steve to put that tape of

24

Slovakian folk music on your ghetto-blaster and fucking blast it out right? Steve, I want you and Steve to break into that bakery over there and start baking blintzes.'

OK, so he was going to get a fucking blintz, or at least he was going to think he was going to get a blintz. And a fucking Slovakian knees-up. But if I'd done my homework correctly, there was no way this cunt was going to be able to resist our trap.

Ten minutes later, as I was tearing the wanker's ear off with a crowbar, I'd been proved right. The plan had gone like clockwork. The combination of the overpowering smell of blintzes and rural Slovakian folk music had proved too much for the cunt. He'd only fucking folk-danced through the police and into our arms. (Truth be told, one or two of the cops were slightly overpowered by the blintz niff, I think they must have been of gyppo descent.) After we'd all had a piece of him, we run him round the back of the bookies so the others who were waiting could have a crack at the cunt. That was one Slovan Bratislavan Czechoslovak tosser who'd be going home, eventually, and telling his mates not to mess with the Chels. Yeah, we'd showed him who was boss.

Later that night in The Cumbucket and Anal Sphincter, we got to thinking about the night's events, about how it had all felt so right. Kicking the shit out of someone cause they support another football team. Yeah, that was what we were all about, that was us.

But there was more. The evening had another

unexpected twist ahead. On the way home after the pub, we ran into a Hendon firm. They were in the Isthmian League at the time (it's now called the Ryman Premier Northern Conference or some shit like that, but it'll always be the Isthmian League to me), but it didn't matter. They weren't Chels so we had to, didn't we? It's like natural selection. If we hadn't, they might've started thinking they were top boys and got above themselves. Then the whole order of things would come tumbling down and before you know it, you won't know where you are without a paddle, you get me? So we fucked them over. Fucked them over good 'n' proper. It was like a bonus, like we'd had our cake and now we got to have the fucking icing too and the fucking cherry on top of the icing.

Yeah, that was the first time I went to football on me own. To tell you the truth, I don't remember much about the football, we never actually went to the game. But it didn't matter cause we got the result we wanted. We had a reputation. We was on the fucking map.

chapter fucking four

At the end of that season, 1974–75, Chelsea were relegated. Course, no one fucking told me, did they? I only found out at the start of the next season, didn't I?

'So, where is it today, fucking Scouseland, or is it the Manc wanks who are getting a kicking?' I said to Steve, flashing my trademark, patented and copyrighted grin at him. Oh yeah, I was a cocky git, a player, know what I mean. I'd worked my way up and now I was a top boy. It hadn't been easy, mind. After the first ten games of the last season, I had to get letters of recommendation from three other top boys, then there were two fucking interviews. Fucking failed the first time, didn't I? They said the geezer I'd glassed in Sheffield had only been in intensive for three days.

Yeah, it was a blow, course. But it only made me more determined. Night after night, I burnt the midnight oil studying. So when it came to the actual games themselves, I was on fire. I gave perfect kicking after perfect kicking. Up at Newcastle one time, I actually got a round of applause for the kicking I gave some cunt. From the Geordies. Yeah, there was no way I was gonna fail a second time, no way. And I didn't. Breezed it. Now I was allowed to wear the real gear, look the fucking business. Went straight out and bought my regulation 90-hole wrought-iron-toecapped DMs. It felt great putting them on. OK, so it took 20 minutes, but it was worth it. I was 11 and already a top boy.

'Naw,' said Steve. 'It's York.'

Now that took me by surprise.

''Ere, Gal,' I said.

'Yeah?' he said.

'Is Steve taking the fucking piss or fucking what?'

'Fucking what,' said Gal.

'What?'

'Well, he's not taking the fucking piss so it must be fucking what,' Gal said.

'Are *you* taking the fucking piss or what, Gal?'

'What, Steve.'

'What?'

'Steve ain't taking the fucking piss and neither am I so it must be what,' he said.

Well, that was fucking it, weren't it? They were taking

the fucking piss, out of a top boy. Chels or no Chels, I couldn't fucking stand for that, could I? I fucking went at them like a killer whale on heat who hasn't been getting any for a while and has a hard-on like a fucking steel girder. Left them in tatters, the pair of them. Cunts. Then I turned to Steve.

'Right, if you don't want to end up like them cunts, you'd better tell me what the fuck is going on.'

'It's like this,' he started.

Well, by the end of it, I had it all clear in me head, like, this relegation thing. It's too complicated to explain in full here, but the bottom line was that we was going to be going to a load of new places, kick in a load of new faces and drink in a load of new boozers. It was the best bit of news I'd had in ages. So off we went to Euston to get the football special to York.

Calling a football special special was taking the fucking piss big style. No it weren't. It was taking the fucking, fucking piss big style. There was nothing special about a football special. They were seething hellholes unfit for fucking animal transportation let alone human transportation. They were filthy stinking turds on wheels, getting us from A to B in the shittest way possible. Course, they weren't like that before we got on. But once we'd smashed all the fucking windows, ripped out all the seats, pissed, puked, wanked and shat everywhere they were. Fucking British Rail.

Anyway, on the train to York, we met up with some of

the other Chelsea mobs and spent the journey chewing over old kickings, looking forward to today's new ones and playing cribbage.

Generally, all the Chelsea mobs got on OK. Well, it made sense, didn't it? You don't hurt your own, unless they're taking the piss like Gal and Steve had been earlier. Or if there's no one else to give a good kicking to. That was where the real camaraderie was. We all knew why we was there, what we was after. If the other lot's mobs didn't show, we knew we could always kick the crap out of each other. And that gave us a bond that went deeper than the deep end at my local swimming pool and probably deeper still.

On this particular day, we found ourselves in a carriage with a mob from Hampstead. They'd let us kick the living fuck out of them last season when there'd been a no-show up at Sunderland, so we were tight. Their top boy was a geezer named Stan. Stan the Man we used to call him cause it rhymed and he was a man, see? There'd been some doubts about him and his bottle in the past. At the last committee meeting, there had even been calls for him to be downgraded to a second-from-the-top boy, but he laid all them doubts to rest by flying to Poland after we got word that some cunt in a Warsaw boozer had been badmouthing the Chels and fucking destroying the gaff, single-handed. That's why he was also sometimes called Stanski the Manski. And Stanoslav the Manoslav. And Stanosovitch the Manosovitch. And Red Stan. And Lech Walestan.

'So what are these Yorkie cunts like, then? They gonna show or what?' I said to Stan the Man.

He eyed me up and down, drinking in my whole being before replying. I've no fucking idea why.

'Yeah, they'll show. They'd fucking better,' he said, licking his lips in anticipation of what lay ahead and cause he was eating a doughnut.

That was Stan the Man all over. Always hoping, always optimistic. For him, the cup wasn't just half full, it was a fucking massive cup that even half full would easily fill a normal-sized cup. But it cost him. Sometimes when the other mob failed to materialise, he'd be gutted, fucking devastated. He'd then go through periods of severe clinical depression before treating himself with tricyclics and the like, cause there was no St John's wort back then, and picking up the pieces of his broken life, ready to try again.

'They will,' I said to him. But I wasn't sure. I just wasn't fucking sure. Basically, I'd lied.

It didn't look good when we got out at York. There was a middle-aged couple with their teenage kids and a party of Italian foreign-language students waiting on the platform. If this was their advance guard, I was not impressed, though one of the Italian students put up a reasonable struggle. I looked at Stan. I could sense that dark cloud moving over him and decided it would be best to remove all sharp implements from him, apart from bottles, obviously.

We walked to the York ground, through York funnily

enough. The place looked like a fucking shithole, hardly even worth turning over, but we did anyway, more to stop Stan slitting his wrists than anything else. Then, it all changed. Tony, a young lanky geezer who thought he was hard but wasn't really as hard as he thought he was, came running round the corner. Yeah, running: that fucking tells you how fucking hard he was.

'Fucking York mob at 12 o'clock,' shouted the bottler cunt.

I grabbed him by the lapels of his shirt and was about to belt him one for fucking running when I looked over my shoulder to see Stan curled up in a ball, weeping down a side alley. He was rocking back and forth, moaning in a low voice, on the very edge of sanity.

'Stan! Stan!' I shouted.

Through great obese fucking tears of utter grief, despair and desperation, he looked up.

'This cunt's only fucking run from the York, ain't he, Stan?' I said, hoping beyond hope that I'd get through to him, somehow, some way.

'Stan, he fucking bottled it!' I screamed.

That did the trick. No need for years of Rogerian therapy and antidepressants. Stan stood up. I could see that old glint return to his eyes. He walked over and grabbed the fucking shitting bottling cunt by the lapels – after I'd let go of them, obviously – and fucking nutted the cunt into next week.

Then Stan looked at me.

I looked back at him.

He continued looking at me.

I continued looking at him.

He looked at me some more.

I looked at him some more.

Then he said, 'What you fucking looking at, you cunt?'

And I knew he was back.

'Let's fucking get 'em,' I said. And off we went. Round the corner and straight into the York mob and a load of York Old Bill, who, truth be told, were more like at 9 o'clock than 12 o'clock like the fucking bottling cunt had said.

We had a field day that day. Every so often, I'd look round and see Stan kicking, punching, biting or stabbing some cunt and it made me feel really good. You see, it weren't all about mindless violence.

On the train back that day, I heard from Larry, one of the generals in Stan's mob, that he'd decided to stay up there for a few days. He reckoned it was just what he needed, to terrorise the city, randomly beating up anyone and everyone he met. The break would do him good and he'd come back refreshed and ready to give the Portsmouth cunts a London welcome they wouldn't forget in a hurry. Yeah, they were next. I had a feeling I was going to like relegation.

chapter fucking five

They say football's a funny fucking old game and even though whoever the fuck 'they' are they're cunts, they're right. That season we had some right old laughs. There was the time that Gal and Gal were laying into some cunt and he shit himself. ''Ere, Steve,' Gal said to me, 'we really are kicking the shit out of this one.' Yeah, there really were some hilarious times but the funniest of them all came when we went up to Oxford.

Oxford, home of the educated cunts. We'd heard their mob were mental, fucking literally. They used the power of the mind to try and win their rucks. Geezer from Blackpool told us. We was having a post-scrap drink in The Combi Boiler and Syphilis with him and some of his mates who we'd just mullahed; cause after the rucking, we was all mates really, what went on during the fighting and that, that was forgotten, there were no hard feelings unless someone died but even then, you could usually have a drink and a laugh about it afterwards. Anyway, this Blackpool wanker got to telling us how they'd come face to face with Oxford's top mob and how they'd started telling them that violence was pointless and that they were just products of their environments and they could better themselves if they really wanted to. You know, really nasty below-the-belt stuff, stuff that fucking hurt. Apparently, it had made some of his lot start to think, and that's the fucking end of it. Once you start to think, you might as well fucking forget it. It's about pure uncontrolled raw fucking instinct. You see the red mist and you fucking go for it. It's mindless violence, not mindful violence, get it? (And I know I've fucking contradicted what I said in the last chapter but if you want to make something of it, fucking come and see me, all right?) Thinking? Nah, that's for nonces and bottlers and philosophers. So we knew we had to be careful with this lot.

Normally, in those days, we'd just get somewhere and assess the situation there and then. Assessing the situation basically meant seeing some other cunts, deciding they were cunts and fucking running them. Well, you don't fucking need much more assessment than that, do you? Course, it's all different now, isn't it? Or so my boy tells me. Now it's all fucking mobiles and Inter-fucking-net and arranging where to meet and doing your fucking week's shopping at the same time. Now, I'm no fucking Luddite, don't get me wrong, I don't even know what the fucking word means, but someone's having a laugh, aren't they? Some of us old boys wanted to go along and watch our kids rucking the other week. There's nothing like it, the feeling of pride you get seeing your own flesh and blood rip the flesh and blood out of someone else's flesh and blood. But could we fucking work out where it was all going to go off? Could we fuck. Only fucking turned up three hours late, didn't we? The young lads fucking slaughtered us for it down The Inverted Nipple later that night. So we gave them a pasting just to make sure they knew we was still the bosses. Come to think of it, there's nothing like the feeling of ripping the flesh and blood out of your own flesh and blood. Kind of made up for the disappointment of not seeing them doing it to someone else.

Anyway, on the way up to Oxford that day, I decided we needed to have a powwow with the other top boys. I got Gal to blow the ceremonial conch that he kept for just such a purpose and we all gathered together. I can picture it like it was the middle of last week, in me mind, like. There was Stan the Man, Nodder, Cretin, By-Tor the Snow Dog, Amblesledge the Rectorian, the Priests of the Temple of Syrinx and, of course, Dr Felchwarden Ph.D., MD, CUNT.

'Right,' I said to the assembled crowd. ''Ere's what I

think. I think if those educated Oxford cunts come at us with their fucking carefully constructed and thought-through notions, we could be in fucking trouble, right?'

'Right,' said Stan the Man.

'Right,' said Nodder.

'Right,' said Cretin.

'Right,' said By-Tor the Snow Dog.

'Right,' said Amblesledge the Rectorian.

'Right,' said the Priests of the Temple of Syrinx.

'Dr Felchwarden?' I said.

'Oh yeah, right,' said Dr Felchwarden.

I never trusted that cunt and something told me to keep an eye on him that day. Or maybe it was Steve that told me to keep an eye on him.

'So, here's what I reckon we should do. If we can't fucking hear what they're saying, they can't fucking hurt us, right? Stands to reason.'

'What if they use fucking sign language, like fucking Makaton or something,' said Nodder.

It was a good point, I couldn't deny it, and I fucking hadn't seen it coming. I needed a comeback and I needed one fast.

'Do you fucking want some, you cunt?' I said.

'You fucking what?' said Nodder.

'You 'eard.'

'Come on, then!'

Then all fucking hell on earth kicked off. We was all going at it hammer and fucking tongs. Apart from Dr

Felchwarden: he just sat in his seat watching the proceedings, knitting and smiling wryly to himself as he stroked the cat that he always seemed to have on his lap even when he was standing up. I don't know what it was but I just knew I'd have to watch him. No, no, it was Gal, he told me to watch him.

Once it had all died down, we carried on.

'Right, this is it. When we get to fucking Oxford, if there's a mob there to meet us, we make a fucking racket so we can't hear what they're saying. Then we make for the first shop we can find and fucking nick a load of earplugs and eyepatches. We stick the earplugs in our ears and keep the eyepatches on us, ready to fucking put on in case they use fucking sign language.'

It was all agreed and ratified without too many more hiccups. There were one or two minor amendments that were discussed, such as if anyone was deaf, they wouldn't have to have any earplugs and if anyone was blind, they wouldn't be requiring eyepatches. Then there was a couple of amendments to the amendments. Cretin wanted to add a line about people who were deaf in only one ear and Amblesledge the Rectorian brought up the issue of what happens should blindness or deafness actually occur during the ruck but before too long it was all sorted. As we pulled in to Oxford, there was a buzz in the air. We knew those cunts thought they were fucking better than us but they were fucking wrong and we were about to prove it.

I got off the train and looked around.

'Gal,' I said.

'What?' said Gal.

'Not much of a welcome party, is it?'

'No. You think those clever cunts ain't gonna show?'

'No, they're gonna fucking show all right. Look,' I said. Gal looked.

'No, not there,' I said. 'There,' gesturing this time.

Fortunately, Gal couldn't read cause if he had been able to, he would have seen a big banner with the words 'Come And Have A Go If You Think You're Intelligent Enough, Though If You're Intelligent Enough You Probably Won't Come And Have A Go'.

'What's it say, Steve?' said Gal.

'Chelsea Poofs Run From Old Ladies With Colostomy Bags,' I lied. I didn't like lying to Gal, though in actual fact I did. He caught me shagging his old lady one time and I told him there was nothing going on between us. Then one time I told him that I was black. This time, though, I didn't like it but I felt it was justified.

The lie had the desired effect. My bullshit made Gal go fucking bat and apeshit. He kicked the banner's fucking head in, leaving it a crumpled heap of shit on the floor. He came out of it pretty unscathed too, just a fat lip and cauliflower ear for his troubles.

We moved out of the station and headed straight for the nearest earplug/eyepatch megastore.

There must have been almost 2,577 of us strutting

through Oxford like we owned the fucking place. Course, a few local youngsters tried to make a name for themselves by having a go. One of them shouted, 'You have real power, use it positively, not destructively,' but before any of the more impressionable of our lot had had a chance to let what he'd said sink in, Nodder despatched two of his boys to kick the living daylights out of the young cunt. He'd think twice before trying to make us think twice again.

Before long, we found the shop. It wasn't any bother nicking the gear, we just went fucking mental in the gaff. But quick, mind. We got what we wanted and legged it before plod arrived on the scene. Then we decamped to a pub round the corner to get tanked up before the big off.

Cause that was all part of it as well, the drinking. It was like the fucking oil, wasn't it? Get that inside you and you're fucking motoring. Back then, see, we didn't know how harmful the stuff was. Like fags in me dad's day, though, come to think of it, it made no fucking difference when we knew they gave us cancer. Made it a bit more exciting in fact. Like taking a risk. Same with fucking drinking, isn't it? You can do your body untold fucking damage drinking but not drinking, that would be like fucking bottling it, so you had to do it, right, cause no one likes a bottler. And cause it was all part of it. Part of the ritual. That cunt Desmond Morris reckons it's all some fucking tribal thing, that we're just fucking doing what

41

our cavemen ancestors did. Yeah? Well where were the fucking dinosaurs? Where were the caves? Fucking wanker. No, granted, there were ritualistic elements to it, but we were far more advanced than fucking Neanderthal cavemen. Bottom line is, it wouldn't have been the same without the drinking and if Desmond fucking Morris wants to make something of that, he can fucking well come and have it out with me anytime. Fucking *Naked Ape* wanker.

The boozer was pretty empty when we arrived, apart from a couple of old boys who scarpered sharpish when we entered; well, as fast as they could with their zimmers. Gal got the round in and after we'd smashed up the pool table and kicked the jukebox to fuck, we sat down for a quiet drink, the lull before the storm, if you like. (There's a fucking expression I've never understood – there's always a lull before a storm, otherwise it would be part of the storm, wouldn't it? A storm is fucking stormy and when there's not a storm it's not stormy so there's a fucking lull, right? I reckon some cunt's having a laugh.)

We'd decided to test the gear we'd nicked. So with the earplugs in and the eyepatches at the ready, we got Steve to shout something at us. Nothing intellectual, like, cause none of us could think of anything like that, but stuff that under normal circumstances would spark us off. Stuff like 'Oi, you're all cunts,' and 'Fucking wankers, think you're fucking hard, do you?' and 'What you looking at, you slag?'

First couple of times, a few of the boys hadn't put the plugs in properly and heard what Steve said so they whacked him. Eventually, though, we had it down to a fine art and he could have been shouting, 'Your mother's a fucking whore,' for all I knew, though if he had been shouting that, I would've fucking killed the cunt (despite it being true). Then he started signing the stuff he'd been shouting and once again, after a couple of false starts with the eyepatches that saw Steve getting belted again, we had it sussed.

But the Oxford cunts weren't called clever cunts for nothing. They'd only been fucking watching us, hadn't they, and the minute they saw that we all had the earplugs in and the eyepatches on, they moved in. Course, Steve tried to tell us but we couldn't fucking hear or see the cunt, could we, and anyway, as the Oxford moved in around us, a couple of quick 'What's it all abouts?' and 'Are you sure this is not just a way of dissipating the anger you feel towards your parents?' and he was floored.

I was the first to take off the eyepatches and earplugs. Immediately, I got hit with a 'Think about what you're doing, take responsibility for your actions' that stung. I knew I had to act and act fast, fucking Oxford were all over the gaff. I roared into them with my glass smashed and ready for action. I took out two of their boys but there were fucking loads of the cunts. An 'Are you a human or an animal?' took the wind out of my sails and

43

I retreated for a moment. There was no fucking way even I could take the lot of them. I needed back-up so I shouted and signed for the rest of the Chels but the cunts still had their plugs and patches in. Quick as I could, I ripped Stan the Man's eyepatches off.

'Stan,' I screamed, 'we're fucking surrounded.'

Course, he couldn't fucking hear me, could he? Before I could start signing to him, I got hit by a 'What's really at the core of your anger?' and a 'You can't fight violence with violence'.

Stan saw me go down and lunged wildly at the Oxford, his earplugs still in. They started desperately signing at him but cleverly he covered his eyes. It gave me just the time I needed to rip the eyepatches off a few more of our boys. The Oxford were now in retreat, some of them even turning to violence themselves. I saw one of them pick up a pool cue but after his mate hit him with a 'Do you really want to descend to their level?', he put it down.

Now we were all over them. In some ways, it was the blind fighting the blind, only we weren't really blind and they weren't at all. In other ways, it was the deaf fighting the deaf. What it definitely was, though, was fucking hilarious. None of us could fucking hear each other and we could only see each other when we uncovered our eyes. A couple of our boys were still sat there with the earplugs in and eyepatches on, totally fucking unaware of the carnage going on around them. The Oxford mob had upped the stakes by bringing in a couple of megaphones but the earplugs held firm and did their job, and when it was all over, when the fucking not so clever now cunts were fucking running down the road, we fucking took to the streets and chased them halfway to fucking kingdom come and then a quarter of the way back. Course, we completely forgot about Steve and Gal still sat in the boozer hearing nothing and seeing nothing. By the time we remembered, we were fucking halfway home. Apparently, they were sat there for fucking hours and when they finally had enough fucking sense to take the stuff off, they only walked out of the pub into a fucking lecture hall where some cunt was lecturing on Marx and the masses. Christ, they took a battering. All that shite about religion being the opium of the people and having had a good time but not tonight. It still makes me laugh to this day. Ha, ha.

chapter fucking six

Over the next couple of seasons, we built up a reputation as the number-one firm. We got respect wherever we went and if we didn't, we turned the place over good 'n' proper. Course, we turned it over good 'n' proper if we got respect as well, otherwise we would only have lost the respect we'd earned and have had to turn it over anyway to regain it. Then Chelsea got promoted again – that's sort of the opposite of being relegated, like – and we were back amongst the big boys. Being in the second division hadn't bothered me cause a cunt is a cunt is a cunt in my book whoever the fuck he is, right, but some of the lads were itching to get back and have a go at the Scousers, Mancs, Geordies, Yids and the like. Yeah, the Yids, even today everyone hates them. Today, when all the fun's been taken out of football by fucking posh poncy toffee-nosed middle-class Eton-bum-boy aristocratic landed-gentry blue-blooded upper-class fox-hunting cunts, you can still have a go at the Yids. They'll never take that away from us.

So we were back where we belonged and we were ready. The summer before the season started, I'd gone on holiday with Gal, Steve, Steve, Gal, Gal, Gal, Gal, Steve and Steve. We'd gone to the Costa del Sol for some R 'n' R: rucking and more rucking. Cause that place is full of cunts. You could normally be sure of it going off on the plane over cause all the big firms used to go out there for pre-season training. Well, it makes sense, don't it? After a summer of no football, you get a bit soft. OK, so there's still fighting in the pub, if some cunt looks at you, if you don't like the look of some cunt, cause you're bored, in a nightclub, with your mates, with their mates, if someone looks at your bird, if someone spills your pint, with squaddies, at weddings and funerals, and if you think someone looks like a nonce, but that isn't really enough to keep you sharp. No, what with dagos as well, the Costa del Sol was a hooligan's paradise.

And it did go off on the plane over, good 'n' proper. Gal had spotted an Arsenal firm down the back of the plane so, being a bit of a looker, he'd shagged a stewardess and then, cause she was now fucking besotted with him, got her to deliver a message to the Arsenal wankers. She went over to them with the food trolley and said, 'Would you like the chicken or the pasta, or perhaps you'd like to look at the special poofs' menu cause you look like soft cunts?' That got them fucking riled. But if that wasn't enough, cause the stewardess bird was now Gal's bird, even though in the interim he'd shagged someone else, he steamed over there and fucking confronted the cunts.

'Oi, you fucking looking at my fucking bird or fucking what, you fucking wankers?' said Gal.

Now the Arsenal really knew something was up. They knew they'd been set up and were going to take a hiding. But all the cunts did was sit there looking gobsmacked, which was exactly what they would be any second.

'Oi, lads,' shouted Gal.

'What?' I said.

'These cunts have been looking at my bird.'

Well, that was like a lot of red rags to a lot of bulls. We all got up and made for the Arsenal cunts. Yeah, it felt great strutting through the plane; walking on air, we were. And all the passengers and crew were on our side. Well, it stands to reason, don't it? No one fucking likes Arsenal. Even the captain came on and wished us luck cause he was Tottenham and he hated the Arsenal cunts.

'Hello, ladies and gentlemen,' he said. 'This is your captain speaking. We're cruising at an altitude of 35,000 feet. We've got a decent tail wind so I expect us to make good time today and get you to your destination a few minutes early. If you look out of the windows to your right, you should just about be able to make out the Pyrenees and if you look to your left, you should be able to see some Arsenal cunts getting the fuck kicked out of them.'

Well, that was like a fucking enormous great red banner being unfurled in front of a whole fucking plain of wildebeest who hadn't seen anything red for a long, long time. It was like that scene in that film *Airplane* where that bird gets hysterical and everyone fucking lines up to give her a slap, only we weren't acting and no one was filming it. Yeah, we taught them a fucking lesson, which was don't fuck with the Chelsea. And just for good measure, we gave them some homework, which was answer this question, you cunts: who shouldn't you fuck with?

So we arrived in dagoland feeling pretty fucking good. Unlike the Arsenal cunts. There then followed two weeks of fucking mayhem by the sea. It was fucking brilliant. We were in ruck heaven. Most mornings, we'd have a ruck in the hotel at breakfast with some wankers who wanted some. Then we'd have a mid-morning ruck, a pre-lunch ruck to get us in the mood for our lunchtime ruck – though sometimes it was hard to tell when the pre-lunch ruck ended and the lunchtime ruck started – an afternoon ruck, a suppertime ruck and of course a fucking massive night-time ruck. Then there were the other rucks that just happened at some time that has no way of denoting it. I mean, it would be fucking stupid to call a ruck the in-between-the-afternoon-ruck-and-supper-ruck ruck or the after-breakfast-but-before-the-mid-morning-ruck ruck. There was even one day when all the rucks just merged into one. I didn't stop fucking kicking the shit out of cunts all fucking day. It was one of the best days of my life. But something was missing and that something was football.

Yeah, football. It just wasn't the same kicking the shit out of someone without football. I don't know what it is. In later life I experimented with other sports. I've kicked shit out of people at rugby games, cricket matches, athletics meets, Grands Prix, tennis matches and at Ascot on Ladies' Day, but none of them matched up to football. So we had to sort out a football match, and that was where Gal came in.

''Ere, Gal,' I said.

'What?' he said.

'You know those dago shitheads you kicked the crap out of at Sparklo del Solo last night?'

'Yeah.'

I knew he'd remember, he had a good memory, did Gal.

'You reckon they'd organise a football match for us?'

'They will if they know what's fucking good for them,' he laughed.

'Yeah, fucking right,' said Steve, who also started laughing.

Then we were all laughing, uncontrollably. Massive

fucking hooligan tears running down our ruddy hooligan cheeks. I don't know what it was, maybe the sun or the greasy dago food or the realisation that everything was futile or some sort of weird combination of the three, but it brought us closer together as a firm and that was a good thing in my book.

When we'd calmed down, Gal went off to sort the dagos out and I went in search of another firm to agree to have the shit beaten out of them at the match.

I didn't have to look very far. As I rounded the corner, I heard the unmistakable sound of a ruck coming from the pub next to our hotel, The Full-Blown Aids. I wandered in to discover that we weren't alone in missing football. It seemed that a firm from West Ham and a firm from Leeds had gone at it over a table football match. The West Ham boys had set themselves up as the red table-footballers firm while the Leeds lads were the blue table-footballers firm. They'd positioned themselves at either end of the table and even got some dago cunts to agree to be Old Bill and try and keep them apart. The game was three seconds old when the West Ham mob ran onto the pitch, or in this case the table, and started offering the Leeds lot out. It had then kicked off when the Leeds top boy had come forward to meet them. The dago police proved to be fucking useless, though the table itself proved very handy as a weapon that was being flung back and forth between the mobs.

Course, I waded in. I had been experimenting with

spitting in rucks and it was a great opportunity to try out some of my newly devised flobs. To be honest, spitting is an art I've never really mastered. I used to spend hours trying to perfect that gob that shoots out between the front two teeth like water from a water pistol or a jet of spunk from a man's penis. Round our way, it was considered de fucking rigueur if you wanted to be a face to be able to sit on a wall and fire one of those gobs out every three to five seconds. My mate Steve was so good at it he became known as Steve the Spitter. But I could never quite get the cunt. It always seemed to fucking elude me. It got to me so much I took a crowbar to Steve the Spitter and destroyed his fucking teeth. We still send each other Christmas cards. The greeny gob was my forte, but in the world of spit that was always a poor second to the in between your front two teeth one. I mean, who can't, with a decent amount of phlegm up, get some distance on a gob? I've even seen girls get ten yards. These days, I've let it go, resigned myself to the fact that I'll never be a great gobber. But back then, I still believed if I really tried, I could make something of myself in the gobbing world. So as I laid into those West Ham and Leeds cunts, I was fucking giving it some with me gob. Cause it antagonises them, don't it? No one likes a yellow pus-coloured lump of lung detritus in their mush do they? Apart from this one bird I knew. But in a ruck, it was like gold dust. It's like the oil that keeps the ruck going. Truth be told, when I waded in, things were dying down a bit but a couple of green goddesses and it all kicked off again. Magic.

So then, when it was all done, I had a word with the two top boys and explained the situation. They were well game. Table football hadn't really done the trick and they were itching for some real football to have a scrap to. The date was set: a local dago park the following afternoon.

'Lads,' I said on my return to the hotel.

'What?' they all said as one, apart from Gal who was unconscious in the bath.

'I've only gone and sorted it, ain't I? Tomorrow afternoon this fucking holiday is going to have its fucking cake and we're going to fucking eat it with one fucking great lump of icing squeezed onto the top.'

It was a good analogy. Or metaphor. Or simile. Or whatever the fuck it was. Cause the lads who understood what I meant went fucking mental with joy and those who were too thick just thought they'd be getting some cake, which made them fucking happy. So everyone was happy, see? Cause that was part of being a top boy an' all, keeping the troops happy. It wasn't just about being the hardest motherfucking motherfucker of all.

That night, I was so excited by the prospect of the following day's violence, I could hardly sleep. I'd even come home early from the nightclub ruck just so I would be good and fucking ready the next day. OK, so I'd brought some German cunts back to the room and had them locked in the bathroom so I could ruck with them when I went for a piss in the night, but apart from that I was going to be well rested and ready for the big off the next day.

The following morning you could sense the anticipation in the air. As I woke up, rolled over and lit up me first fag and cracked me first can of beer of the day, there was a strange, eerie silence, broken only by a low Prussian moaning coming from the bathroom.

'Can it, Bismarck, you slag, or I'll fucking start the Third World War on your face, you fucking shit-eating scumbag,' I shouted. That was one German cunt who wouldn't be first to the sun lounger or terminally unfunny or extremely methodical or whatever the fucking stereotype was.

The other lads started to come round, apart from Gal, who was still unconscious in the bath, and we went down for our breakfast ruck.

'Now listen, lads,' I said, 'I don't want you to go soft on any cunts this morning, right, but remember we've got a big off this afternoon. Make sure you teach them a lesson, but leave it at that, right?'

They didn't need to be told again; they were as excited as I was about the afternoon in prospect. And as I watched them rucking over breakfast I knew they'd listened to me. I saw Gal kicking some lanky geezer's head in but just as he was about to pull the cunt's tongue out and shove it up his nose, he stopped and nutted the fuckwit once more before leaving it.

'Good lad,' I thought to myself in my head.

That day, time seemed to drag like it was losing a tug of war very, very slowly. My mind wasn't really on the job during the other rucks and I knew it. And I knew the others knew it too. But then I knew that they knew that I knew they knew it so that was all right. Finally, it was time for the big one.

Just like we would back home for a real match, we all gathered in a boozer, The Tit and Enema, near the park/ground before the game. As we were turning it over, Steve ran in.

'Oi, lads,' he shouted.

'What?' we said.

'There's a West Ham firm that have joined forces with a Leeds firm and they're coming down the road heavy-handed.'

OK, so we'd set it up, but it was having the desired effect. The adrenalin was pumping and squirting and jizzing and sploshing and whooshing and shooting all over the place. Some of the lads had even injected themselves with extra adrenalin just to give them an extra rush.

'Right, Gal, Steve, Gal, Steve and Gal, you go round the back. We'll meet them head on and chase them round to you. Got it?'

As one, they all nodded. But just then, Gal came running in with an unexpected development.

'Lads,' he shouted.

'What?' we said.

'A fucking dago firm's only gone and got itself tooled up and is coming this way an' all.'

They all looked at me, then quickly looked away before I could say 'What the fuck are you looking at?' and kick the shit out of them. This was the unexpected development that I mentioned a few lines back and it was a tricky fucker. Cause there was no fucking rule book, no fucking manual telling you what to do; that's what this cunt is, right? The problem was this: who did we fucking hate more, the West Ham/Leeds firm or the dago cunts? To put it another way: who did we fucking hate more, the dago cunts or the West Ham/Leeds firm?

I weighed up the pros and cons. The dago cunts were foreign, that was a big con, no doubt about it. The West Ham/Leeds firm were a West Ham/Leeds firm, that was also a big con. I was back to square one. Time was running out. I knew I had to act and act fast.

'Gal,' I said.

'What?' he said.

'If you were kicking the shit out of a West Ham cunt and some dago prick came along, would you stop kicking the shit out of the West Ham cunt and start kicking the shit out of the dago prick?'

I knew it was pointless asking Gal, he was a thick cunt, but I was stalling.

'I'd stop and start giving the dago cunt a hiding,' said Gal.

Well that fucking threw me. I'd expected Gal to be all

over the fucking place with that one. But no. The cunt had acted on instinct, pure hooligan instinct. His brain had kicked in with the answer, the involuntary, knee-jerk, primeval answer. The cunt didn't even know he'd said anything. You see, behind his thoughtless answer, the thinking was this: we're all British, right? When we go away with England we stand and fight together against the dago wop kraut bastards, then when we get back home, we kick shit out of each other. It was simple, I couldn't believe I hadn't seen it. But now that I had, I knew exactly what to do.

'Let's get the dago cunts,' I screamed.

And out the boozer we piled, headlong into the dagos. And like the dago cunts they were, they fucking run like the little-fucking-girl cry-baby poof cunts they also were. We chased them into the fucking sea that day. Not one of them stayed and had it out, not even their top boy. As for the West Ham/Leeds mob, they'd fucking started having it out with each other on the way to the match. Kicked shit out of each other, which was well out of order. Well, it would have left us out on a limb if the dagos hadn't showed. Yeah, we wouldn't forget that next season in a hurry all that much.

chapter fucking seven

As summer turned into nearly the end of summer, we saw the fruits of our labours on the Costa paying off. We started that season on a high that would carry us right through until fucking Easter. We were like that arrow at the start of *Dad's Army*. Fucking going all round the country – or as I like to call it, the cuntry – hand-delivering personalised kicking in after kicking in, with no cunt stopping us. It got to the point that smaller firms would come and watch us just so's they could take notes and learn. A couple of them even asked me to be a guest speaker at their annual conferences, but I told them to fuck off. Yeah, I know, it was stupid; I could have been making a tidy living on the after-dinner circuit now if I'd thought about it, but back then all I wanted to do was fucking ruck, not fucking talk about rucking.

But I'd be lying if I said we had it all our own way. Don't get me wrong, we were the most feared firm in the country, end of. But after coasting through the season, that Easter we got something of a comeuppance. And it still fucking pisses me off to this day cause it was just sheer fucking stupidity and complacency. If I could turn the clocks back, I wouldn't have been so stupid, though I might still have been so complacent. But, apart from one hour every year, I can't do that so I'll just have to live with it.

It was gearing up to be the biggest weekend in the hooligan calendar. There was an FA Cup semi-final in town featuring the Geordies, the Yids were entertaining the Scousers and we had the pleasure of West Ham's company. Yeah, the very same cunts who'd let us down on the Costa. It was payback time and they were going to be paid back with interest of around 8.9 per cent APR, which was fucking high for the time considering it was the era of the three-day week and the milkmaids' strike and Black November and all that.

Chelsea–West Ham has always been tasty. Not just cause they're fucking east London scum who reckon they're the fucking bees knees and who come over to our manor with their fucking east London ways. No, there was more to it than that and there always will be. It goes back to the fucking '50s, don't it? Yeah, the '50s. A time when some cunts would have you believe there was no trouble at football, that it was all fucking 'Excuse me, chum, but you're in my way, would you mind awfully standing to one side' and 'Oh, not at all, chum, terribly sorry and all that'. Yeah, well that's fucking bollocks, right. Trouble and football have been fucking synonymous since football began. There's even a school of thought that says football was only invented so we could have a decent ruck. Now I don't fucking know about that but I do know it first kicked off when Wanderers played the Royal Engineers in the FA Cup final back in fucking 18-something-or-other. But it wasn't reported, was it? Cause they didn't have *The Sun* back then, it was all *The* fucking *Times* and that, and all they wanted to know about was whether fucking Colonel Cunt Bollocks-Shithead was getting engaged to Lady Hairy Fanny-Fuckballs, wasn't it?

Anyway, this one time, West Ham were well out of order. Me granddad told me about it. Well, he wasn't really my granddad cause I never knew my real granddad, obviously; he fucked off long before I came around, long before anyone came around for that matter. It was the geezer I called granddad that told me, the old boy who was knocking off me mum at the time. He must have been 90-odd if he was a day but he could still give her a slap when he needed to. Come to think of it, I should probably have called him great-grandad and called the other geezer me mum was seeing at the time granddad but that's easy for me to say now, with the benefit of fucking hindsight and no speech impediments and that. Anyway, even though he was an old cunt, his memory was fucking razor sharp. If you told him to fuck off down the shops and get your beer and fags, more often than not he'd come back with both.

It was during a league match in 1958. Both teams were in the First Division North or whatever the fuck they called it in those days. Back then they had their own dress code, didn't they? It was all flat caps and grey flannel suits with camel-hair or vicuña overcoats and bermuda shorts and rattles. But it was the flat caps that were the most important things. Cause when there was a goal, they had to throw the fuckers up in the air, right? Yeah, can you fucking believe that? Stupid old cunts. Course, when some historian tosser looks back at our time, the cunt'll probably say that we were fucking stupid an' all but I'll tell you this, if he fucking comes round our way and says that, he'll get a fucking hiding and no fucking mistake. So, this game, right. A firm of West Ham had infiltrated the Chelsea that day. It wasn't difficult, they just fucking walked right in cause they had Chelsea rattles, didn't they? They had to remember to keep fucking shtum though. Any of that fucking rhyming slang or spoon playing and they'd be sussed and given a right fucking going over. So, they're in amongst the Chelsea and they're fucking waiting. Waiting for a goal. And they don't have to wait too long. Six minutes in and Chelsea fucking score. All the fucking hats go up in the air like the fucking Pavlovian response that it was but do they come down? Do they fuck. The West Ham firm have only gone and tooled themselves up with fucking peashooters and they're shooting peas at the hats to keep them in the air. Well, in anyone's book, that's bang out of order. The Chelsea look fucking stupid, they look like fucking mugs in their own back yard. But without their hats they can't do nothing, can they? It's like if a policeman comes to nick you without his hat on, he can't, can he? And the West Ham cunts kept the hats up there for the rest of the game. So when Chelsea scored again, which they did, three times, grown men were tearing their own fucking hair out and pulling their ears off just for something to throw up in the air. It was right fucking pitiful. And all the time the West Ham are laughing cause they can laugh and shoot peas at the same time, see. Now, that sort of going over you don't forget and, apart from Gal who needed reminding every so often, we hadn't forgotten. So there were plenty of scores to be settled that weekend.

'Gal,' I said.

'What?' he said. He was in a bad mood that day.

'If we work this out proper like, I reckon we can have a row with the fucking West Ham cunts, the Scousers, the Yids *and* the Geordies, and then come back for another go at those fucking West Ham cunts again cause one hiding ain't nearly enough for those cunts after what they did to us in the Costa and in the '50s.'

'What was it again that they did in the '50s?' said Gal.

Like I said, he needed reminding but after I did, he was fucking up for it double time. If he'd've sniffed out a fucking bubble-blower there and then, he would've killed the cunt. Well, he would've killed them anyway but that day he would've killed them some more.

So we had it all worked out. We were going to have the fucking West Ham cunts at Victoria, then leg it round to King's Cross on the District and Circle Line to have the Geordies and the Scousers, head down to fucking Finsbury Park on the Victoria Line for the Yids and then get back to Fulham Broadway by going on the Victoria Line to Victoria and then changing to a Wimbledon train on the District and Circle Line to hammer the fucking Hammers again. It wasn't going to be cheap, mind – don't forget there were no fucking travelcards in those days – but it was going to be money well spent in our book.

Setting off from Dollis Hill, which was still on the Bakerloo Line then, we had the sun on our backs and on our faces when we turned round, and the wind in our hair and also on our faces as well when it changed direction.

'Single to Victoria, please,' I said to the coloured girl who worked in the ticket office.

'That'll be 35 pence please, sir,' she said to me. I handed over a pound in folding, cause that's another thing we still had back then, got me change and we were off to a series of massive offs. Or so we thought. As we travelled down to Victoria, there was only one thought in our collective mind: West Ham. We could smell the cunts, but by the time we'd finished with them they wouldn't be able to smell us cause their noses would be fucking shattered and cause we'd all had baths that morning.

Pulling in to Victoria we roared out of the carriages. I remember looking at Steve as he raced up the escalators and thinking, 'I'm nearly out of fags, I must remember to get some later.' Then we were out on the main British Rail concourse and ready for them. Only the cunts only weren't there, were they?

'Fucking bottling cunts,' screamed Gal at the very apex of his voice.

But I knew better. Whatever they were, and they were many things like cunts and wankers and tossers and slags and chartered surveyors, West Ham weren't fucking bottlers. No, something was up.

'Gal,' I said.

'What?' It was Steve, he'd thought I was talking to him.

'No, not you, you cunt, Gal,' I said.

'Oh, sorry,' said Steve.

'What?' said Gal.

'This ain't right, something ain't fucking right, it's wrong, all wrong.'

I was thinking out loud – speaking, really – but I

needed to work it out. This was the big one and it was looking like we were going to miss out. Then it hit me like a fucking great sledgehammer in the mush.

'That's fucking it!' I shouted. 'King's fucking Cross. Come on!'

That was the stupid and complacent bit, right there. I'd assumed that the West Ham cunts would be coming through Victoria to get to Chelsea and normally they would have, but they were looking to have a fucking go at the Geordies and Scousers as well, weren't they? So they'd be going via King's Cross. I felt like such a cunt. It really was a low point.

'Fucking give me a good kicking, lads,' I said.

It was a throwback to Nutter's days, when he'd fucked up.

The lads looked at me. They knew I needed to feel physical pain to take away the mental anguish I was feeling right there. Cruel to be kind, it was, as they laid into me.

Four broken ribs, a fractured jaw, depressed skull, detached retina and three stab wounds later, I was feeling much better.

'Right, if we're fucking quick,' I said, 'we can still make it to King's Cross for the big off.'

With renewed vigour we raced back down into the Tube again.

'Single to King's Cross,' I said to the geezer in the ticket office.

He looked at me like I was some sort of cunt but I kept it buttoned; I knew better than to fuck with a London Transport official.

'That'll be 25 pence,' he said.

And we were off again. This time I could smell not just the West Ham cunts but the Geordies and Scousers as well. And Steve, who, it turned out, hadn't actually had a bath that morning, the filthy cunt.

We had a laugh on that train journey. There used to be a sign above the doors in the train that read 'Obstructing the doors causes delay and can be dangerous'. So we only fucking rubbed out bits so it read 'Obstruct the causes can dangerous', didn't we?

But that was just a side issue compared to the real pudding. Arriving at King's Cross, we were out of that train like fucking lightning. Apart from stopping so a couple of Japanese tourists could take our picture, we didn't stop for no cunt. With a roar of 'Chel-sea', we surged out onto the King's Cross mainline station. Like a massive shoal of really hard fish, we moved around the platforms trying to sniff out the West Ham and Geordie and Scouse cunts. But the fuckers weren't there. I had a massive sense of already seen. (I'm fucked if I'm going to use fucking Frogspeak.) And as we turned in to Platform Eight, we knew we'd missed it. The place was a fucking ghost town, it was Hiroshima, just after the bomb, not before, or now. There was all the evidence of a major ruck having taken place – weeping bystanders who'd been caught in it, teeth, broken bottles, various limbs and hysterical Arabic women ripping their garments and flailing their arms about their heads maniacally. We were too late.

'You know what to do, lads,' I said with all the fucking dignity I could muster.

And they didn't let me down, piling in like they fucking hated me, which some of them probably did. Cause I'd let them down hadn't I? And they looked up to me like the fathers, stepfathers and foster fathers none of them ever knew, and in some cases the mothers. So I had it coming.

'Right,' I said, wiping blood, snot, bone marrow, bits of flesh and crack cocaine from my nose, 'this is our last chance. If we get back to the Bridge in time (we might still) be able to have it out (with) those West Ham cunts. And fucking come out looking like top brass.' (And if you're wondering why the fuck I put brackets in there, it's because I can cunt, OK?)

This time no one said a word, but we all knew what it meant. The game at the Bridge was being fucking televised, wasn't it? It'd be on *The Big Match* the next day. If we put up a good show on the terraces, we might just be able to save the day. Cause for all the talk that goes round the hooligan grapevine, you can't argue with cold, hard pictures of violence. I mean if some cunt tells me that the Yids took the North Bank at Highbury and gave the Arsenal boys a good hiding, well, I've only got that cunt's word for it, ain't I? And seeing as how he's a cunt, I'm inclined to think he's fucking lying. But you see me fucking ripping the head off West Ham's top boy on *The Big Match*, there's no fucking getting away from it, is there? Yeah, there was an extra buzz when the cameras were there. And they loved it too, the television companies. Oh yeah, they had a nice little side earner going. They used to sell copies of the rucks to S&M clubs in Soho so that fucking pervs could get off on seeing us rucking. In fact, I became something of a celebrity amongst the S&M fraternity. So, there was hope, and with that hope came belief, and with that belief came energy, and with that energy came one thought: 'Let's fucking get those West Ham cunts.'

'Single to Fulham Broadway,' I said to the ticket office official.

'That'll be 25 pence, please,' she said to me. I handed over the money. She handed me the ticket. It was all over in a matter of seconds.

Down on the train, we had more laughs with that sign, changing it to 'doors can be and dangerous'. Some of the other passengers had a right laugh at that, but we were too uptight to give them a kicking. Piling out at Fulham Broadway, we were like an unruly tribe of savages. Yeah, I'll admit it, some of our discipline had gone, but we were desperate.

We ran down the Fulham Road towards the Shed, Chelsea's notorious 'end', so called because it looked like a shed and it was at one 'end' of the ground. Flying through the turnstiles, our fists were already clenched, in my mind I could already hear the crunch of knuckle on tooth, the doof of forehead on nose and the twock of boot on head. But as it turned out, that's all it was, in my mind, because what I could really hear was laughing. Yeah, fucking laughing. All around, people were fucking pissing themselves.

'What's so fucking funny, you cunt,' I said to the nearest cunt.

'Ah ha ha ha, you are, ha ha ha, a ha ha ha, a ha ha ha, a ha ha ha, a ha ha, a ha,' he said.

Needless to say, once I'd ground his fucking nose into the concrete with my 120-hole platinum-toecapped DMs, he wasn't laughing any more. Only, he was. Even with his face half fucking splattered all over the fucking terraces, he was still laughing. Well, not really laughing. It was more a mixture of cries of terrible pain with just a hint of a titter in there, but it was there. I didn't fucking get it.

'Gal,' I said.

'What?' said Gal.

'Something's not fucking right here, something is not fucking right!'

'You're fucking right, something is not fucking right.'

That made me feel a bit better, that I was right about something not being fucking right, but something was still not fucking right. Looking up to the top of the Shed, I saw West Ham's top boy fucking wetting himself. I made a beeline right for him.

'Oi, you fucking east London scumbag, do you want some?' I said, spitting the words out so that some spittle hit the cunt in the eye.

'No, I don't,' he said. 'Cause I've already had some.' And then the cunt fucking cracked up. Fucking laughed like he was on laughing gas and stoned and being tickled all at the same time. It was too much. I had no fucking idea what the cunt was on about, but I knew enough was enough. Just to make me feel a bit better, I nutted the cunt and then took my cock out and pissed on him, but I knew it was time to leave with what little self-respect I had left. With the guffaws of the assembled mob still ringing in our ears like a bad case of tinnitus, we trooped off.

I remember sitting in the boozer that night watching the rucking going on all around me and barely having the energy to join in. I just didn't get it. I was replaying the day's events over and over, but nothing came to me.

'Come on, Steve,' said Steve. 'Don't bottle it up, let it out, you'll feel much better.'

And he was right. Picking up the table and throwing it at some cunt did help a little. As did throttling the bastard with some electric flex and pulling his teeth out with my teeth, but at the end of the night, I was still left with a sense of fucking confusion.

The next day, even me mum was worried about me.

'Come on, son, how about I help you kick shit out of your brothers this morning, eh? That'll make you feel better.'

'Fuck off, you slag,' I said back to her. That stopped her worrying a little and we ended up having a ruck ourselves, but she was still concerned. She even wanted to ring the fucking doctor, but I wouldn't let her out of the headlock I had her in so she couldn't do it.

Then, all was revealed. I turned the telly on to watch *The Big Match* and there, there I fucking was getting the living shit kicked out of me. Plain as fucking day. Only it wasn't fucking me, was it? The fucking West Ham had set it all up. They'd fucking dressed up one of their mob to look like me and taken him to the fucking cleaners. Kicked the crap out of the cunt. Apparently, he was on a life-support machine. Brian Moore had a fucking field day, didn't he? 'Terrible scenes,' he said, and he was right as far as I was concerned because whoever it was that was really getting a kicking, *his* reputation wasn't in tatters. No, mine was. It was a blow, a fucking big blow and I knew there and then, give or take ten minutes, that things would never be the same again. I was wrong about that, but I was going to have to fucking work some to regain my crown as Britain's top top boy.

chapter fucking eight

I'd wanted to go to the World Cup in Argentina in 1978, but me mum wouldn't let me, which normally wouldn't fucking bother me none, but I was only a fucking kid then and couldn't quite yet kick the fuck out of her so she got her own way. Spain in 1982 was a completely different story. By then, I had pubic hair and hands the size of big hands so there was fuck all she could do about it. It was just the chance I'd been waiting for to re-establish myself, in front of the whole fucking world. It was perfect. They didn't get *The Big Match* in Spain then so the dago cunts would only have that summer we'd spent there to go on, and that meant they'd still fucking respect us. Course it's all fucking different today. If I was still at it today and West Ham made me look a mug, which isn't going to fucking happen right, but if they made me look like a hypothetical mug, it'd be halfway round the fucking world before I could say 'cunt' and then it'd be fucking released on DfuckingVD (or D syphilis as we call it round our way) on some fucking hilarious compilation called *Football's Bad Boys* and hosted by Danny fucking Baker or Angus fucking Deayton or Nick fucking Hancock and priced £12.99 and available from all the usual retail outlets. No, I was going out there and I was going to fucking show the world who was boss.

I suppose you could say that I was helping to spread what some journalist cunts called 'the English disease'. Yeah, well, that was one way of looking at it, but I preferred to see it as a chance to kick shitloads of shit out of shitloads of fucking foreign cunts without having to travel round the fucking world. I mean what the fuck is the difference between doing it in World War Two and doing it at the World Cup? If anything, less people got hurt at the World Cup than in World War Two, though I don't have the official statistics to back that up. No, I missed out on the almighty ruck that was World War Two; there was no way I was going to miss out on this one.

Following England is an interesting fucker. As I said back in chapter whatever the fuck it was, there you are standing shoulder to shoulder with some cunts who, if it was on your own patch, you'd be laying into, only you're all on the same side now so you're not laying into them, you're laying into some foreign cunts, see? Together. It can be a mindfuck and no mistake. Some people can't fucking deal with it. One week, they're giving this cunt a battering, next week, they're fucking helping him batter some other cunt. Stan the Man couldn't handle it. Well, he wouldn't would he, what with his bi-fucking-polar disorder and that. He went out to Norway during the qualifiers and freaked out. Kicked shit out of a mob from Swindon, a mob from Lincoln and a Norwegian girl who looked a bit like a face from Aston Villa. He was deemed not just out of order but well out of order and bang out of order. Because of that, a few firms got together and put forward a proposal that we have our own qualifying competition to see which firm would go out and represent England on the terraces. Never fucking happened though, did it, cause they all fucking knew who would win, end of.

Nonetheless, it was decided that before we all went out there we should have some bonding sessions. Gal couldn't fucking believe it.

'Bonding sessions!' he said.

I didn't mind though, I could see the benefit of it, though a big part of me couldn't.

We all moved into this fucking great caravan park in Whitley Bay and took it in turns to be foreign cunts. When it came to my turn, I didn't much like the idea.

'I'm not fucking being a foreign cunt, pretend or otherwise,' I said.

'No, I'm not fucking eating no dago shit,' said Gal.

'I'm not fucking wearing no cunting beret,' said Steve.

'I'm not fucking talking no wog language,' said Gal.

'There's no way I'm going to fuck another geezer up the arse,' said Steve.

Well, that was that, wasn't it? In the end, it was agreed that we would still be a Chelsea firm and the other lads would be the foreigners come to have a go at us, only on their turf, abroad, like. It worked a fucking treat cause not only did I hate the cunts anyway, now that they were pretending to be foreign, I hated them even more. I ended up hospitalising four lads from a Preston firm who were pretending to be Ghanaian. We still keep in touch from time to time.

After the bonding session, we were fucking more up for it than ever. I still hated all those other cunts, and there'd be no special treatment for any of them next season, but when your country needs you, you have to do what it takes, right? We're not a Chelsea firm or a Manchester United firm or a Derby firm then, we're an England firm. Course, if things didn't pan out, and the foreign cunts didn't play ball, we could always kick shit out of each other, but we knew that wasn't going to happen.

We set up camp in some dago shithole; Seville, I think it was called, or some other fucking stupid name. The locals welcomed us with open arms, for about three fucking seconds. Then, when the first one of them had taken a fucking boot to the head, they turned and ran. They wouldn't make the mistake of welcoming the English with open arms again.

There were several camps dotted all around Spain and one in Belize, and in order to keep all the lads up to speed about which cunts were getting a bit fucking mouthy and needed sorting out, we had to rely on a complex series of coded messages that were hidden in the speeches made by prominent dago politicians of the day and non-mobile telephones. Neither were ideal, but they worked and that's all that mattered.

'Ring, ring.'

It was the telephone.

'Get that, Gal,' I said, knowing full well that he would.

Gal sat up and walked over to where the ringing sound was coming from which was also where the telephone was.

'Hello,' he said. 'Yeah. Where? When? How many? Not with my skin condition. Bye.'

It was the big one we'd been waiting for. England had beaten France 3–1 in their opening game, and even though we'd given the Frogs a right going over outside and inside the stadium, and outside and inside some nearby houses, and outside and inside a local bullring and outside and inside a Kentucky Fried Chicken, we knew it wasn't over, not by a long chalk.

'It's on,' said Gal.

'Where?' I said.

'Oh shit, I don't know, I forgot to ask,' said Gal.

'You did, you stupid cunt, I heard you,' I said.

That jogged his memory all right, and before long we had all the information we needed and some that we didn't, like why Gal's mum had to have her ovaries removed the previous October.

It turned out the fucking dago police were only going to help the fucking Frogs. Foreign cunts sticking together, that was what it was. But that was fine. I didn't differentiate between Frogs and dagos and krauts and wops and spics. They were all foreign cunts to me, and if they wanted to help each other out, all the fucking better cause they'd all get a battering together.

The word was that the Frogs were gathering in some boozer in town, Los Urinas Auriolos (The Golden Shower). They'd run some Bubbles out and were lording it up all over the place, giving it plenty with the old mouth. Apparently, they were saying things like 'Oh, the Eeengleeesh, zay sink zay are, 'ow you say, le bollocks de la chien' and 'Ooh la la, we will do ze cancan on ze heads of ze Eeengleesh cunts.' Not speaking a word of French, I didn't have a clue what it meant, but I didn't need to. I knew it meant they were taking the fucking piss, and that was not just bang and well out of order, it was seriously out of order.

It was Gal who came up with a plan.

'Let's go down there and fucking kick the shit out of those cunts,' he said after some thought.

'Yeah!' said Steve.

'Yeah!' said Gal.

'Yeah!' said Steve.

'Yeah!' said Gal and everyone else.

It was a good plan, but something, something didn't seem right.

'Wait a minute,' I said.

Then, exactly 60 seconds later, 'Don't you see, that's just what those cunts're expecting us to do.'

They didn't see and neither did I to be honest, but I had to say something, otherwise I'd look a right cunt. A geezer from Derby, Fraser, he did get it, though.

'So let's wait,' he said.

'Exactly,' I said.

So we did. For three days. Then we made our move.

Walking into town at the head of a seething mob of English, I felt like the man, the main fucking man. I felt like William the Conquerer and Genghis fucking Khan all rolled into one. Course, a few other top boys were up front too, but I was always one step ahead of them, literally, so I really was the one at the head and they were more like at the neck or shoulders.

'There's nothing I like more than battering French cunts,' said Gordon, a top boy from Leeds. He was better known as just 'G' and he was a main face. I had a grudging respect for the cunt cause of the battles we'd had in the past and cause he was the only openly transvestite hooligan in Britain at the time. Course that doesn't count for much nowadays, but back then, it took guts to kick the shit out of someone wearing lacy knickers, a miniskirt and a silk blouse. I also knew that I might have to rely on him and his boys if things took a turn for the worse.

'You look nice,' I said.

He blushed, his face turning a deep shade of ketchup.

As we walked on, the adrenalin began to really pump. My heart started to thump like it was a punch-bag and I was hitting it. It was a fucking buzz, and I felt happy to be alive. Unlike those French cunts, who would be happy to be dead by the time we'd finished with them.

As we entered the square where the bar was, it was like a scene from a Western except without the horses. The place was fucking deserted apart from the bar. Word had got out that we were coming, that was for certain, or everyone had gone on holiday or they all had to be somewhere else at that precise moment for some reason. Whatever the fuck it was, it made our life that little bit easier. Cause in my book there's no such thing as innocent bystanders. If you don't want to get involved, you should fuck off out of it. If you're there, you're fair fucking game. But some of the lads didn't like the thought that some people – women, children, the mentally handicapped – might get hurt when they were just passing through or watching or something. And that put them off a bit. So it was good that there were no other cunts around. It focused our attentions on the job in hand.

I walked up to the front door of the bar. I could hear the Frog cunts inside.

'Fucking hell,' said G, 'it stinks of fucking garlic.'

Everyone roared with laughter. A couple of the lads got

the giggles and became hysterical. But that was G all over, always the funny man (or woman).

Then from the back of our mob, I heard an unmistakable sound that I wasn't about to mistake. It was the sound of water cannon against flesh. The dago police were laying into us from behind, soaking our rear guard. I had to do something, and quickly. If it carried on, too many of the lads would have to go back to the camp and change into dry clothes. But before I could do anything, the fucking Frogs only came piling out of the bar, didn't they?

'So, we meet again, you Eeengleesh peeg,' said their top boy, garlic oozing from his every pore and coming out of his mouth like it was trying to fucking escape from a garlic-eating monster in his fucking stomach. I nearly gagged.

'You want some, then?' I said.

'Oui,' he said.

'Yeah,' I said.

'Oui,' he said.

'Yeah,' I said.

'Oui,' he said.

'Yeah,' I said.

Then it got nasty. The cunt pulled out the longest-looking blade I'd ever seen. Now, I wasn't averse to a blade. I'd cut up many a cunt before, it was a tool of the trade, weren't it? I mean, there's nothing like the feel of warm fucking cranberry juice spurting over your hand as you plunge the blade into some cunt again and again and again and again and again in a frenzied, furious attack.

But this one looked like it could really do some damage. If ever I needed my bottle it was now, and thankfully, it didn't desert me.

'Call that a blade, you cunt?' I said, as a few droplets of water landed on my cheek. The dago police were closing in. I was staring the cunt right out. I knew he was rattled. He readjusted his beret and pulled up the string of onions round his neck so that they were almost choking him.

'My cock's bigger than that,' I said. 'On the fucking flac.'

And then I fucking hit the cunt. He went down like a sack of potatoes weighed down with cement. He hadn't been expecting that. Well, he probably had really, in terms of the things that he might have been expecting it wasn't that unexpected, but the cunt reckoned he could take it, didn't he, and that was his mistake.

Seeing their top boy crumble like that sent shock waves through the Frog mob. They turned to run back into the bar, but it was a Thursday, wasn't it? Half-day fucking closing. In the interim, the owner had only shut down for the day, hadn't he? They were fucked and they knew it. As we laid into them, I sent Gal and Steve and a Brighton mob off to sort out the dago police. They took a right soaking, wet through they were, and none too pleased about it.

'You fucking drips,' said T-Bone, a Carlisle lad with a wicked sense of humour.

We all had a laugh at that one.

'Yeah, you old soaks,' said Ringo, a face from Rochdale who wasn't very funny.

No one laughed at that one.

Back at the camp that night, we relived the day's events, literally. Gal, Steve and the Brighton mob weren't too happy about getting soaked again. There was even a bit of a stand-off between them and the Sheffield firm who were acting as the dago police, a stand-off over and above the one they were reliving, that is, which pissed me off, to tell the truth. I mean, if you're going to relive a day's events, you've got to stick to the fucking script, right? See, there were rules to the game we were playing. Break them and you're a cunt. And that made Gal, Steve and the Brighton mob cunts in my book. And the Sheffield mob. So that night I went to bed in a bad mood. It still fucking niggles me to this day when I think about it, so I try not to. But memory's a funny cunt, isn't it? That night as I was dozing off, I think I remember G coming up to me and whispering, 'Is it really bigger than that blade on the flac?' But I may be wrong about that.

chapter fucking nine

Like the England football team, we fucking walked it through the first phase of the World Cup. They were unbeaten and so were we. Unlike the foreign bastards there, who were beaten fucking black, blue, indigo, violet and orange. The second phase brought a new challenge though: different foreign bastards. For some reason, in the first phase we'd only kicked shit out of other European firms, a kind of Eurovision Shit-kicking Contest. (Definitely France nul points.) Now we had some new cunts to deal with: the South Americans. Brazil and the fucking Argies were the only two teams from that part of the world left in the tournament, but they weren't the only two South American firms still around. The El Salvadorians, the Peruvians and the Hondurans had stayed in Spain. They'd mainly kicked shit out of each other during the first phase, but now, like the cunts they were, they'd decided to band together as one big South American firm and offer out the rest of the world. And that, cause we'd kicked ginormous great lumps of crap out of everyone else, meant us.

It was a challenge, make no mistake, and our first task was to assign our new enemies names, cause apart from the Argies they didn't have none. 3T, so called because he weighed 15½ st., a middle-going-on-top boy from Colchester, got the ball rolling.

'The way I see it,' he said, 'it's like this. Some cunts' names come from their name, like Pakis and Argies, and some don't, like dagos and krauts and wops. So we either use part of their name or we don't.'

He had a CSE in metalwork, 3T, and I think he lost some of the other lads.

'Eh?' said Gal.

'You want me to stick one on 'im?' said Steve.

I did and I didn't. There was no doubting 3T had been something of a cunt with his high-fucking-falutin ways, but he also hadn't been a cunt in that he'd been trying to help out only he'd gone the wrong way about it. It was a tough call, but in the end, I gave Steve the nod.

'Right, so what are we going to call the Brazilian cunts?' I said, as Steve kicked 3T's teeth in.

'Cunts,' said Gal.

'Yeah, like it,' said Steve.

It was good, really good, I had to admit that, but it wasn't quite right.

''Ere,' said Gal, ''ow about, cause, like, they're all fucking dagos really, right, calling them, like, Brazilian dagos.'

That was what I liked about Gal, every once in a while that one fucking brain cell of his started to work. That and the fact that he never forgot my birthday. Then I heard a whimper coming from beneath Steve's boot. It was 3T. Desperate to make amends, he made another suggestion.

'What about putting the names together and calling them Bragos,' he said, coughing up three teeth.

There was silence. You could have heard a flea fart. I was thinking about what he'd said. Fuck knows why the others were quiet.

'What about the Peruvians?' I said, dribbling spit onto his forehead.

'Pergos,' he spluttered back.

'And the Hondurans?' I said, pissing in his mouth.

'Hongos.'

'The El Salvadorians?' I said, biting his ear lobe off.

'Elgos.'

'Let him go, Steve,' I said, 'the cunt's redeemed himself.'

Steve wasn't happy about that, but there was nothing he could do about it. Or rather, there was nothing he could do about it that wouldn't see him get the living daylights kicked out of him by yours truly, so, knowing what was good for him, he left it.

With the names of the South American cunts sorted, we now had other things to think about.

The thing about the South American firms was they scrapped in a different way to us. It was like their football teams. They were all fucking skill and fancy shite, playing the game to a fucking samba rhythm and all that, not caring about defence cause they knew they could sort it out up front. So when they rucked, they fucking didn't do it the English way, going at it hammer and tong, kicking the absolute fucking brains out of whatever cunts they happened to be having it out with. They were all fancy punches, and deft kicks and perfectly placed head-butts (Rio kisses). And they'd fucking move like they were fucking dancing. Pirouetting around you as they cut you up. If you ask me, it was fucking poof fighting. Yeah, they did damage, but it wasn't meant to be fucking art, this wasn't *Swan* fucking *Lake*, this was hard cunts having it out, man to fucking man, not man to fucking ponce. So there was a whole rucking philosophy at stake here as well as everything else, which was mainly them being foreign cunts.

It was all set up to go off at the Brazil–Argentina game. One fucking dago spic cunt looks like the other so the Hongo, Pergo and Elgo cunts would have no problem getting in. It wouldn't be so easy for us though. We were faces now, and arms and legs and torsos, the whole fucking caboodle. If we were spotted, the dago police would form a human pyramid around the ground and prevent us getting in. So we had to travel incognito. Back then, there was no Internet or nothing to help us research what these cunts looked like. We had to rely on television crowd pictures from previous games. By the look of them, the Brago cunts were the ones to go for. They tended to paint their faces in the team's colours, play the bongos and have a few birds dancing around, mostly with big titties. Recruiting the birds was no trouble. We were top boys, sharp, good-looking lads, a catch for any bird, foreign or otherwise. For the promise of some English cock with a view to marriage, a move to England and a chance to escape the stinking shanty fucking towns they lived in, the dago birds would do anything. Deep down, they probably knew we wouldn't fucking touch their dago cunts with a fucking bargepole sheathed in a giant condom, but they allowed themselves to dream, even if it was only for a few hours.

The bongos and face paint turned out to be no problem either. Ace, a semi-face from Bolton, sorted that. His old man had been a main bongo dealer before he was murdered by some rival bongo dealers. Ace had inherited a warehouseload of the fucking things and they'd just been gathering dust. This was a chance to put them to good use and avenge his father's murder; well, the former, anyway. And on his way to the warehouse, he passed a paint shop, so he could pick up the paint an' all. It all fitted into place perfectly, almost too perfectly. Truth be told, I'd have preferred it if it had fit into place very,

very well instead of perfectly, but if it was to be perfectly, then perfectly it was to be.

Decked out in the gear, we got into the ground no problemo. We'd even had a drink with some Brago and Hongo cunts in a boozer before the game. The muppets only didn't fucking cotton on, did they? Well we were all speaking the universal language of drink, so they wouldn't have, would they? We still contrived to nearly blow it, though.

'Fucking hell, I've got to lamp one of them cunts and I've got to do it now,' said Steve, after he'd performed a credible lambada in front of a circle of clapping onlookers.

'Yeah, come on,' said Gal, 'what are we waiting for? Let's kill the cunts now.'

'Shut up, you slag, and have another cigarette,' I said, shoving a packet of Benson & Hedges into his hand.

It was a gesture, but not an empty, idle one, a full, active one.

'Keep a fucking lid on it, lads. If we plough into them now, it'll be all over before you can say "my ostrich is convalescing". And there are no fucking cameras here to catch it. So keep it fucking locked, you cunts. This is where the whole fucking world gets to know who not to mess with.'

I was becoming quite the philosopher in my old age, and the lads knew when to take me seriously, which was all the time when I was dealing with slags and cunts and foreign shitheads.

Apart from that slight wobble, our pre-match preparations went off without a hitch. In fact, we'd blended in so well that when we set off for the game, some of the big-titted dancing girls begged us to let them come along, something we were more than happy to let them do, as it would give us a huge advantage over our foe and because they had big titties. It was an advantage that we needed cause we were probably outnumbered roughly thirty-four to one, approximately.

By the time the game kicked off, we were neatly ensconced between an Elgo firm and some Argies. The Bragos had taken the opposite end of the ground, and the Pergos and Hongos were dotted around elsewhere. There'd been sporadic outbreaks of violence, but we'd even planned that so as to lull them into a false, almost imaginary, other-worldly sense of security. Let them think that we'd turned up and they'd already sorted us out, that was the logic behind that one. Only they hadn't bothered to see the logic in front of it, had they? Now it was just a matter of getting the timing spot on.

Ten minutes into the game, the timing was spot off. Twenty minutes in, it was still spot off. But with half an hour gone, it was definitely spot on. I told the lads to spread out amongst the South American cunts and wait for my signal. Gal took up position next to some ugly Argie cunt, Steve took up position next to some ugly Hongo cunt and Gal took up position next to some reasonably good-looking Brago wanker. Gyrating towards the big-titted dancing girls, I slipped an arm around the waist of one of them. She smiled at me, but not for long. Lifting her up above my head, I shouted, 'Eng-ger-land!' at the top of my voice and lobbed her into a mob of Argies. At that, all merry fucking hell kicked off, apart from where Gal was, as he hadn't realised that was my signal.

The South American cunts were stunned, and we also had another advantage that we hadn't foreseen. By blending in so well with the cunts, we'd only picked up some of their fancy fucking fighting skills, hadn't we? So when they tried to hit back, we were equal to them. It was a fucking riot, literally. The dago police piled in with tear gas, pepper spray, mustard gas (English and French mustard), boiling oil and taramasalata. The South Americans scattered all over the terraces, running like the bottling faggots they were. Course, we run after them, didn't we? And we caught them. I grabbed the Elgos' top boy and fucking winded him with a punch to the stomach. As he fell to the ground, I fucking kneed him in the teeth. Then as he lay on the ground, I jumped up and down on his head. Then I sat on his back and pulled his head back before smashing it on the ground over and over and over again. And then, just for good measure, I gave him a Chinese burn and pinched him really hard.

By now, I was really cooking. It was almost as if the spirit of Nutter was driving me on to be more and more violent.

It was like he was saying 'Go on, son, kick the fucking cunt in,' and 'Fucking twat the bastard, good lad.' Bollocks, I know, cause I didn't even know if he was dead or not, but it didn't matter, somehow I knew he was looking down on me. Maybe, deep down, that's what I'd wanted him to say to me when he was around, but if I could pretend that his spirit was watching over me saying those things, that was good enough for me. Better, in fact, cause the real cunt would never have said anything like that.

That day, we really hit the big time. Pictures of us rucking went around the world with a message, and that message was 'Don't fuck with us or you'll get fucked.' Course, seeing as how we were dressed like Bragos with our bongos and big-titted birds, Brazil only got the fucking blame, didn't they? FIFA, the governing body of world football – I've never managed to work that fucker out, surely they should be GBWF – fined the cunts by making their national rate of inflation 600 per cent. But, halfway through the ruck, making sure a camera was filming me, I rolled up the sleeve of my Brago disguise to reveal an armful of swastika tattoos so that those who knew who it really was knew who it really was, if you get me. And they also knew who the top boy was. Me. Myself. I. I had returned and was on top of the fucking world. The rightful order of things had been restored to its rightful order, and it felt fucking great. But back home, storm clouds were brewing and it defi-fucking-nitely wasn't tea they were making.

chapter fucking ten

In the dictionary, hooliganism is defined as 'acts of vandalism and violence in public places, committed especially by youths'. It comes from the Latin *hulium*, to batter, and *ganos*, some cunt. In the early '80s, I would have added to that definition 'predominantly English youths'. Yeah, other countries had their firms, but if you believed what you read in the press, we were the only hooligans worth our salt. Like the telly cunts, they loved us, the press. We gave them more column inches than Nelson's Column. Course, most of what they wrote was fucking shite. One time, there was an account of a ruck that went off between us and a Millwall firm at a dinner party in Knightsbridge. The fucking journo cunt wrote, 'The thickset burly chap who clearly seemed to be leading the Chelsea supporters threw a wild punch with his left hand, a punch that, had it connected, I feel sure would have caused considerable damage to its intended victim.' Bollocks. I threw that punch with my right hand and that journo bastard knew it as well. He was just trying to make a name for himself, wasn't he?

So we were getting written about all the fucking time, and that meant that those middle-class cunts in their middle-class streets in their middle-class houses eating their middle-class meals of middle-class food on middle-class plates with middle-class cutlery were fucking talking about us in their middle-class voices. Yeah, the cunts. Cause they weren't having proper conversations about us like 'Fucking hell, Torquil, Chelsea gave those Burnley cunts a right seeing to, didn't they?' and 'Yeah, Claude, they fucking run 'em all over their own back yard, the cunts.' No, it was nothing like that, it was more like 'I say, Torquil, these football hooligans are becoming something of a nuisance, aren't they?' and 'Yes, Claude, it's about time the authorities did something about them.'

Well, there was no way the Government could cover their ears and go 'nah, nah, nah, nah, not listening' to that. Once the chattering cunts start chattering they've got to do something or they're out on their fucking arses, aren't they? That's why at the start of the next season we only fucking found ourselves the subject of a sociological experiment, didn't we? 'Violence and Football: An observational study to assess the underlying causes of hooliganism.' I mean, fucking hell, if that didn't take the biscuit, I don't know what did take the biscuit. We were only asked if we wouldn't mind some sociologists from Leicester University coming with us on our rucks to study our fucking behaviour. Steve couldn't fucking believe it.

'Study our fucking behaviour!' he said.

At first I wasn't having none of it.

'Think about it,' I said to the boys one night down The Eggplant and Woofter. 'If we've got these fucking sociowhatsit cunts hanging around us all the fucking time taking measurements and getting out their fucking test tubes and Bunsen burners and that, that's going to severely cramp our style. I mean, how can I kick some cunt's head in while some other cunt's fucking taking a sample from my DMs, eh?'

'Yeah,' said Gal. 'How can he kick some cunt's head in while some other cunt's fucking taking a sample from his DMs?'

'No, I'm going to write to the cunts and tell them they can take their fucking socio-fucking-logical experiment and stick it where the sun don't fucking shine, and that doesn't mean they can stick it anywhere they like during a total eclipse.'

So that's exactly what I did.

Steve Fist
Top Boy
Chelsea Firm
Dollis Hill

Sociology Department
Leicester University
Leicester

Dear Sir,

I'm afraid my colleagues and I are going to have
to decline your offer to use us as the subject of
your study, as, if you think about it, if we've got
these fucking sociowhatsit cunts hanging around
us all the fucking time taking measurements and
getting out their fucking test tubes and Bunsen
burners and that, that's going to severely cramp
our style. I mean, how can I kick some cunt's
head in while some other cunt's fucking taking a
sample from my DMs, eh?

Yours etc.,
Steve Fist

I remember sending that on the Tuesday. There was a pre-
season friendly against the Mick side Glentoran the
following Saturday; friendly for the players maybe, but
there was no such thing as a friendly for us, and clearly the

sociology boys were keen to be there at the start cause I only fucking got a letter back from them on the Thursday.

> Sociology Department
> Leicester University
> Leicester

Steve Fist
Top Boy
Chelsea Firm
Dollis Hill
Dear Steve,

Thank you for your letter. While you clearly make some very salient points, we would like to assure you that our intention is in no way to hinder your activities. Aside from some initial interviews, we would attempt to blend in with you and your colleagues, making our observations 'incognito' and allowing you to carry on your day-to-day activities as before.

Yours etc.,
William Johnson
Dean of the Sociology and Inhumanities Dept
Leicester University

So that was their fucking game. They wanted to be part of the number-one firm in the fucking world. They wanted their top sociology boys to come and muscle in on our firm, after which they'd no doubt go back to their fucking sociology mates and mouth it off about running with the Chels. Well, at first I wasn't having none of that either. I mean, we'd come up the hard way, us lot. You want to be part of our firm, you've got to earn the right.

But then I had second thoughts. Yeah, we'd earned the right to call ourselves top boys, but in our world. They were top boys in their world, or at least that's what I reckoned. So we was on a par. I mean, there was no way they'd send a fucking second-rate sociology firm to observe us. Or would they? That's when I had third thoughts.

Now I was really fucking thinking; fourth, fifth and sixth thoughts came along rapidly. What if they were fucking using us to become top boys in the sociology world? They could be the cunts of the sociology world who got lucky. And that would mean they were taking the fucking piss. And if they were taking the piss, they'd get what's coming to them, like any other cunts who take the piss.

'Yeah,' said Steve. 'They ain't nothing special. If they've got what's coming to them they'll get what's coming to them.'

'Yeah,' said Gal.

Then we had a right old sing-song. 'In your sociology slums, you find a dead cat and you think it's a treat, in your sociology slums.' And 'You're going to get your fucking sociology heads kicked in' (claps x 10). So, like any off, we were one step ahead of the cunts. Ready to fucking mullah them if they stepped out of line. And if they didn't, we'd probably mullah them anyway.

They turned up, four of them, on the Saturday morning before we set off for the Glentoran game. To be fair to the cunts, they'd made a real effort to try and fit in. Over their white lab coats they were wearing all the gear that the well-dressed football hooligan wore in the early '80s – Tony Benster shirts, Crook jeans with their floundered pockets and festooned turn-ups, shiffle-boaters, silk drifters and, of course, DMs. They'd also had their left ears pierced, which meant they weren't fucking poofs. Their names were a problem though. Professor Hartley Hocktweed-Japseye, Professor Terrian Deforestation, Dr Ethelred Byzantium and Tobias Spit. It wasn't a problem for long though.

''Ere,' said Steve. 'Why don't we call the cunts Gal, Steve, Gal and Steve?'

'You are fucking showboating, today, mate,' I said to Steve. Then we hugged like two long lost brothers, which for all we knew we might have been. Cause there was a fucking camaraderie there. These were my fucking mates. They'd stuck by me season after season, battering after battering, cunt kicking-in after cunt kicking-in, bastard bashing after bastard bashing and slag slashing after slag slashing. OK, so we might have been putting it on a little for the sociology cunts, yeah, fair dos, but this was the start of a new season, and, having finished the last one on a high that was fucking mentally high up, we were looking down on the rest of those cunts saying, 'Come and have a go if you think you're hard enough, but make sure you do some altitude training first.'

That first match, the sociology mob showed us their mettle. Apparently they'd been having it out with the psychology boys, the combined studies boys and the media studies boys in preparation, and they'd clearly done their homework. I wouldn't say they were rock hard exactly, more like pebble hard, but they used what they had well and worked as a team. And they were willing to learn. After that Glentoran game, we all sat down in the The Shit Shovel and went through the day's events.

'So, if I understand you correctly,' said Professor 'Gal' Hocktweed-Japseye, tugging excitedly on his bow tie, the adrenalin from the day's rucking still pumping around his 63-year-old body, 'kicking the living shit out of someone and mullahing some cunt are fundamentally the same thing, whereas giving someone a slap or twatting them is something different.'

'Fucking hell, Prof,' I said, 'they don't call you Prof for nothing. But look, words ain't really our thing, so let's give you a practical demonstration. Gal, give that cunt over there a slap.'

Gal duly went over and laid one on the cunt who was drinking quietly in a corner.

'Right,' I said. 'That was a slap, see. It's like a warning, isn't it? It says, step out of line and there's more where that came from.'

'I see, I see,' said Prof Gal. And I could tell from the way he'd written down every word I'd said that he did get it.

'Now then, this is mullahing some cunt.'

The lads then laid into the cunt, did him good 'n' proper. Well, it was for scientific purposes, wasn't it? A couple of the sociologists videoed it, and then, cause they'd forgotten to video the cunt getting a slap before, we propped him up so he looked conscious and redid the cunt getting a slap so they could have that on video too to show their mates and at conferences and that.

'Well, I must say this is all very interesting,' said Prof Gal. The other three all agreed. It was then that I realised Prof Gal was their top boy. I'd have to keep an eye on him. Top boys are top boys in anyone's language, and we can be right cunts when we have to be. I reckoned he wanted a fucking Nobel Prize or something for this and would do whatever it took to get it.

Then came the interviews. The sociology firm asked us all sorts of fucking questions about our backgrounds and what we thought was right and wrong, and when it was right or wrong to do it if it was right or wrong. Course, we lied right out of our arseholes, didn't we? Told them the biggest load of bullshit since bullshit was invented. They only fucking lapped it up, didn't they? Like cats drinking a bowl of fucking cream, only the cream wasn't what they thought it was, but they didn't know that. That's why at the end of the day they concluded that us people who are violent at football come from homes with two loving parents one of whom used to think he might be bisexual but is now sure he's hetero. Generally, both parents worked long hours in the felt-tip pen industry and had tattoos on their upper limbs but not below the navel. Oh, and they found some evidence to suggest that eating Marmite was a contributory factor. We had a fucking laugh about that, didn't we? They never knew about it to this day, so if you're fucking reading this now, Prof Gal, if you're not dead, that is, or senile, we made you and your mates look like right fucking mugs and no fucking mistake.

But to give them their dues, they stuck by us that season. Chelsea were wallowing in the Second Division, looking like they might even drop down to the Third – something we couldn't fucking countenance cause even though it meant different places to go to and different cunts to batter like I said before, it wouldn't take much to run the likes of Scunthorpe, Lincoln and Darlington, disrespect intended, and that would mean we might lose our touch.

We had some decent rucks that year, at Wolves in particular. They think they're hard cunts up there, and thinking you're a hard cunt is halfway to being a hard cunt (the other half is not thinking you're a hard cunt). But the sociology mob fucking waded in no problem, even when a Wolves firm fucking outnumbered us three to one. I can still remember Prof Steve fucking turning round and saying, 'Come on, you cunts, let's fucking have them,' before fucking going at it with one of their top boys and taking notes at the same time. To tell the truth, I felt right fucking proud, like I'd done something worthwhile. OK, they weren't total amateurs when they first came along, but there was no way back in August they'd have had the bottle or the front to do what Prof Steve did that day. I'd never have fucking admitted it at the time for fear of being called a fucking gay poof, but there was a lump in my throat at the end of the season.

'I have to say, and I think I speak for all of us,' said Prof Gal, 'it has been a most engaging and invigorating experience, three and half million pounds of taxpayers' money well spent.'

'Yeah, well, make sure you don't fucking forget the lessons we taught you. If I hear of you bottling it from any other academic cunts, I'll fucking come round your way and tear you apart.'

I was putting it on a bit cause really – inside, like – I wanted to sob and wail and let all the hurt out.

'Actually, I've been meaning to ask you a favour,' said Prof Gal.

His timing was spot on; I'd have done anything for the cunt then, apart from let him bugger me up the arse or suck me off.

'An article has just appeared in one of the more prestigious sociology journals criticising an article I wrote last year. I was thinking of going to see the chap who wrote it to discuss it with him, but now I feel it might be more instructive if we were all to go along and sort the cunt out.'

So that's how I found myself on a university special going up to Warwick just after the end of the season. Turned out that their sociology department fancied themselves a little. Well, we fancied them a lot and didn't have the time to have it out with them through the pages of various academic journals. This was going to be sorted out, and sorted out good 'n' proper.

We piled out of the train at Warwick expecting some sort of welcoming party, but even the local Old Bill were acting as if they weren't bothered by us.

'Fuck me,' said Gal. 'This is gonna be a fucking doddle.'

'Yeah, this is going to be easier than fucking taking QPR,' said Steve.

QPR were legendary in the hooligan world as being fucking no-hopers. It always seemed odd to me, seeing as how the area they were in was not particularly noted for its soft-as-shiteness. At the time, there was a theory about it: that being so close to the headquarters of the BBC, their firm was paid to be mickey mouse so that the fucking TV cunts could get the pictures of us real hard cunts doing what we do best – fucking kicking the cunt out of other cunts – without having to go too far off of their own manor. See, when we went down QPR, we always gave them an extra-fucking-hard kicking cause they were so shit-soft. Like I said, the firms that put up a good fight gained our respect, which didn't mean we went easy on them, no fucking way, but when you smell fear on some cunt – and it's a strange sort of smell, a mix between lavender and shit – that's when you really fucking go for it, and we smelt a fuckload of fear on the QPR cunts, and vinegar.

Personally, I wasn't so sure it was going to be as much of a doddle as Gal and Steve reckoned. I knew that word of our arrival would get back to the sociology department at the university. They weren't going to miss 200 Chelsea strutting through the centre of town chanting 'No surrender, no surrender, no surrender to the Warwick University sociology department'. No, those cunts would know we were in town and they'd be ready for us.

In fact, things kicked off sooner than we'd expected. We stopped in a boozer to whet and wet our appetites and chanced upon a group of visiting professors from the University of California, Los Angeles, or UCLA as the cunts insisted on calling it. Prof Gal was straight in at them.

'What do you think about Truseau's critique of Durkheim?' he said.

'It's not bad,' said one of the UCLA cunts, 'but if you'd care to have a look at the next issue of the *American Journal of Sociology*, you'll see I refute a number of his basic arguments quite comprehensively.'

Well that was it for the Prof. The fucking red mist descended and he laid into the cunt. Course, we backed him up. As they scattered, I saw Steve grab a pool ball and ram it down the vice-dean's throat. They were no match for us and it was all over pretty quickly, but it was a good warm-up for the main event.

Walking onto the university campus, we split into two groups. I didn't normally like to do that cause it meant putting Steve in charge of the other group and then he might get ideas above his station, but it was necessary in this situation, and anyway, I made a mental note to kick the shit out of him at some later date just to keep him in his place.

The professor we were looking for was called Vincent Wells and apparently he was hard as fucking nails. His firm of dedicated field researchers and technicians were feared throughout the sociology world, and for good reason. Their theories about the nature of society and group dynamics were rock solid. Every time anyone had anything negative to say about them, they took a fucking battering, leaving their reputation in tatters. Not knowing a fucking thing about the cunting subject, we made the decision to do our talking with our fists, a decision that, with the benefit of hindsight, and at the time, proved to be the right one.

Professor Wells was taking a seminar group of third years in his rooms. But we never got that far. My hunch that people were clued up about our arrival proved to be correct and as we strode towards the rooms, university security staff, local police and some of the Prof's research team appeared at the end of a corridor to meet us. A pig-ugly cunt who clearly fancied himself came forward, eyeballing me as he did so.

'This is as far as it goes, chaps,' he said, still eyeballing me.

I eyeballed him back.

He eyeballed me some more.

I eyeballed him some more back.

He tried to eyeball me even more, but a trickle of sweat rolled into one eye which meant that he could only eyeball me with one eye to my two. He knew he was fucked.

I grinned that wide grin that said, 'This is as far as it goes, chaps? You're fucking taking the cunting piss, aren't you, mate? And no one fucking takes the piss out of me, least of all some cunt like you, have you got that, you cunt?' (Believe me, that's a fucking wide grin.)

I love that moment before it all goes off, that delicious moment when it's all waiting to happen, hanging in the air. Sometimes I used to toy with that moment, stretching it out just that little bit longer. Other times I just waded in and fucking went for it. This was one of those moments. A sharp blow to the stomach winded the cunt, and a knee to the jaw as he went down – shattering his chin in 364 places – made sure he wasn't getting up again.

The local Old Bill tried to hold their ground, but we surged through them, taking a few down as we went, and headed for the Prof's rooms. When we burst in, it was like the *Marie* fucking *Celeste*.

'Fuck!' shouted Prof Gal, clearly annoyed.

'Bollocks!' shouted Prof Steve, also clearly annoyed.

'Trebor Mints!' shouted Dr Gal, not so clearly annoyed.

But I wasn't annoyed. Walking over to the window, I looked out over to the central courtyard where Steve and the other half of our mob were giving Prof Wells and his band of by now very unmerry students a fucking seeing to. I knew they'd fucking leg it when they heard the commotion going on with the police – not so fucking hard when it came to fighting with fists and sharpened two-pence pieces as opposed to pen and paper. That's why I'd taken the risk with Steve's self-esteem and sent him off with the others, to fucking cut them off, and it had worked a treat.

Prof Gal and the others charged down there and had a field day on Prof Wells' face, and the rest of his body for that matter. Cut him up good 'n' proper. Six months later when the cunt could write again, a full retraction of his article was published and Prof Gal and the honorary Chelsea sociology mob were officially named as top sociology boys. And they only returned the favour, didn't they? I was invited up to Leicester Uni to receive an honorary sociology degree, quite a good one in fact, a 2:1. It came in very handy when I was caught short going up to Sheffield the following season.

chapter fucking eleven

We'd always had a pretty good relationship with the Old Bill. There was a sort of mutual respect between us, you see. They were good cunts and we were bad cunts, but we were all cunts, you get me? Yeah, they'd nick a few of us in the early days, give us a going over, a fat lip, a cauliflower ear, an aubergine nose, a pak choi cheek, a torn rectum, the usual stuff. But we knew they were only having a laugh; you could tell, and anyway, Steve told us. He was a copper himself, see. Kept it quiet of course, from the press and that, but he wasn't the only one. A lot of firms had coppers who ran with them. I knew of two firms that had assistant chief constables among their number and one who had the third most senior copper in Britain as their top boy. (I'm not the sort of cunt who names names, but the geezer is now a senior stylist at Toni and Guy's in Nantwich.) He was a fucking hard nut an' all. I got cornered by his mob up at Derby one time. He gave it all the 'Right, mate, I'm going to have to take down your particulars and smash your fucking face in at the same time', cause I knew who he was and he knew I knew it. That's not to say he got any favouritism. His crew were up at Crewe one time having it out with the Crewe crew. The local boys in blue, the Crewe boys in blue, only fucking nicked the Crewe crew and held them down so that this geezer's crew could lay into them. Well, he was having none of it. Fucking ordered his boys to lay into the Crewe coppers and threatened to talk to their senior officer about it. After that, him and his boys was treated just like any other hooligans. When he was being a hooligan, that is; they still all sucked up to his fucking cock when he was in uniform poncing around all the inner cities with some politician cunts and that.

So, yeah, on the whole, things were sweet with the law. Until they weren't. Until the whole fucking country went apeshit about us having a good time. I mean, it's not as if we objected to other cunts having fun, is it? What if we'd fucking said we didn't like cunts dressing up in New Romantic gear or some other shit that was going on at the time? Would they have got the Old Bill to try and sort that lot out? No fucking way. That's why there was a lot of bad feeling when the coppers started turning the fucking screws on us.

It was 1983. I was already a legend in hooligan circles. I was no longer Nutter's son. No longer Nutter junior, little Nutter, wee nutty Nutter the bastard offspring of Nutter. No. Now *I* was Nutter. Reborn and fucking ten times worse. A hundred times worse. I could have had Nutter no fucking problem. If Nutter had come up to me and said, 'Oi, Nutter, you fucking want some then?' I would have said, 'Yeah, any time, you slag.' Right enough and no fucking mistake an' all. Course, he might think he'd have a psycho-fucking-logical edge, being my father, but that would be his biggest mistake, after thinking he could have me and offering me out, which were also mistakes but not as big as that one. I would fucking kill the cunt, no two ways about it. People used to shit themselves when I was around. I was fucking evil incarnate, whatever that means. Which of course is why the Bill came looking for me, wasn't it?

We were having a drink in The Tampon, me, Gal, Gal, Gal, Gal and Steve. We were playing Swansea on Saturday and were looking forward to fucking teaching the Taffs a lesson they wouldn't forget in a hurry, but also wouldn't remember in a hurry either cause of the fucking brain damage we were going to do them.

'I fucking hate Taffs,' said Gal.

'Yeah,' said Steve.

'Yeah,' said Gal.

'Yeah,' said Gal.

'Right,' said Gal.

'Why do you hate Taffs?' I said. I was playing with them, toying, they hadn't expected that. Gal was getting nervous. I could see the fear in his ears.

'Cause they're fucking Taffs,' he said.

'So if I was a Taff, you'd fucking hate me?'

It was like playing with a kitten, only this kitten was going to get its fucking head ripped off.

'Nutter?'

The voice had come from behind us. Instantly, there was the sound of three chairs being pushed back and one sofa – cause Gal, Gal and Gal were sitting on a sofa – as we stood to face our unknown assailant.

'You fucking what?' I was ready to explode, to fucking tear this cunt who had come into my boozer and said my name from limb to fucking limb and back again, via more of his fucking limbs.

'DI Carnegiehall, and this is DC Youngvic. We'd like a word if you don't mind.'

They flashed their fucking ID badges in front of my nose, like I gave a shit. A cunt with a badge is still a cunt whichever way you look at it and if these cunts were looking for trouble, they'd come to the right place.

'We're not looking for trouble,' said the first cunt.

'Shit,' I thought, 'they're not looking for trouble but they've come to the right place. It's like us looking for trouble but going to the wrong place. It could only mean one thing: trouble.'

'You'd better sit down then,' I said, not taking my eyes

off them, which was tricky seeing as how there were two of them.

To be fair, they did sit down, though they sat down on the sofa which meant Gal, Gal and Gal had to stand.

The cunt who had spoken first spoke first.

'It's like this, Nutter. Things have been sweet between us, right?'

'Right,' I said, because it was.

'We've let you carry on with your fights, stabbings, slashings, glassings, sadistic beatings and torturings and all that, right?'

'Right,' I said, cause it still was.

'And for the most part, we've turned a blind eye, a deaf ear and a blocked-up nose. Yeah, we've been seen to do what we had to when we had to, but you and I, and DC Youngvic and all your mates and most of the people in this boozer and all the other firms up and down the country, we all know we was just giving you a slap on the wrists to keep the cunts up above happy. Right?'

I thought about it for a while.

'Right,' I said.

'But now things . . .'

'Right,' I said.

'Wait for me to finish, you cunt,' he said.

'Right,' I said. He carried on talking. But now I wasn't listening. In the back of my mind, a voice was going, 'Hang on, did he just call me a cunt? He only fucking did, you know. That fucking cunt of a shithead copper just called me a cunt. In front of my mates. That is crash bang wallop out of order.'

By now, the voice had reached the front of my mind and the fucking red mist was coming down in what was more like red hailstones. I stood up and heaved the fucking tableload of drinks all over the cunt.

'No one fucking calls me a cunt, you fucking cunt,' I screamed. And then I was on him, on his lager-sodden body, kicking fucking great lumps of shit out of him. And his mate. The two of them went down like the fucking wastes of space they were. You could hear the crunch of nose bone being decimated by my boot as far away as fucking Neasden, probably as far away as Wembley Park if your hearing was particularly good or you were a bat. By the time I'd finished with them, which was about 9.30, they were as useless as a fucking camel in an igloo.

'Now get out of our pub. Woe be-fucking-tide you or your cunt of a mate if I ever see you in here again.'

'This is war, Nutter,' said Carnegiehall, spitting out bits of teeth and fillings and expensive bridge-work as he crawled towards the door. 'Your days are numbered.'

But I didn't give a shit. So now there was another firm out there to ruck with, that's all it meant to me.

'What a cunt that fucking copper was,' said Gal.

'Yeah,' I said. 'So, if I was a copper, that'd make me a cunt in your eyes, would it, Gal?'

I could see that fear in him again, smell it, taste it,

touch it, caress it. But then I smiled and I saw the fear drain out of the cunt like it was hot air in a hot air balloon and a giant me had stepped on it. I'd had my fun with the coppers, see. I'd give Gal a kicking another day.

'Something tells me Swansea's going to be a fucking laugh now,' I said.

'Yeah,' said Steve.

'Yeah,' said Gal.

'Yeah,' said Gal.

'Right,' said Gal.

And it only fucking was – fun and a half. The following Saturday, we boarded the special at Paddington. We were well up for this one and already in high spirits as we'd run into a New Romantic firm on their way to buy the new Duran Du-fucking-ran album and given them a fucking run for their money. It wasn't union with a snake, it was union with my fucking fist and they legged it like fucking girls (on film). But somewhere between the back and the front of my mind, the words of that copper were ringing in my head. I wondered what he meant by 'war'. I didn't think he meant mobilising the armed forces and attacking a neighbouring country. Or repelling an invading force using land, air and sea battalions.

'Tickets, please,' said a voice that didn't sound like Gal, Gal, Steve, Gal, Steve, Steve or me.

'Fucking hell,' said Gal.

'Jesus fucking Christ,' said Steve.

'Bollocking fuck monkeys,' said Gal.

'Fuck me sideways with a greased up stepladder,' said Steve.

This was a fucking mind-fucking-fuck. In all our years of travelling to away games on football specials, we'd never once been asked for tickets. Some of the lads didn't even fucking know what tickets were.

'Is this cunt having a laugh or what?' said Gal, talking about the ticket inspector.

We all laughed. Gal stood up.

'You want my ticket, do you? Well, here it is.'

Gal put his hand in his pocket but when he pulled it out again, he didn't have a ticket in it, he had made it into a fist. Somehow I knew what was going to happen.

'Stop!' I said.

Gal looked at me. The others looked at me. The others looked at Gal. Gal looked at the others. Some of the others looked at me again and some of them stayed looking at Gal who was sort of half looking at me and half looking at the some of them that had stayed looking at him.

'Here,' I said to the ticket cunt, and handed him tickets for all of us.

'That's lovely, sir,' he said. 'Enjoy the match now, won't you?'

And then he was gone, into the next compartment, where I just heard him say 'Tickets, please' before being slashed by a Stanley knife.

They were all looking at me now.

'Are you all fucking looking at me? Come on, then, you cunts, you and me, now!'

And then all fucking hell kicked off as I shit-kicked my way through Gal, Gal, Steve and all those cunts whose arses I'd just saved and who were so fucking ungrateful about it. Cause I always bought tickets, see, just in case; just in case some cunt came along and fucking said 'Tickets, please'. And, yeah, maybe it would have been easier to give him a slap and tell him to fuck off out of it, but sometimes the easy way is not the best way.

Once it was all over, I took Steve to one side.

'Listen, mate,' I said.

'Yeah,' he said.

'That was just the fucking start, all right?'

'Right.'

Cause now I knew what that cunting copper had meant. Now I knew they were going to fight their petty fucking war with petty-minded middle-class fucking bureau-cunts trying to get in our fucking way. Ticket inspectors, turnstile operators, lollipop ladies, Old Bill. The cunts would use whoever they could to get at us. As the train pulled in to Swansea, I saw a fucking welcoming committee of Taff Old Bill swarming around the platform like a rain-cloud of fucking locusts. And I could see the cunts grinning, giving it that moronic Taff grin (not dissimilar to my wide grin, truth be told, though with perhaps less clenching of the teeth and more dribble).

'Right, lads,' I said, 'they've put on a bit of a show for

us. I think it's only right and proper that we put on a show for them.'

The lads grinned back at me through the bruises I'd given them. Not the moronic grin of the fucking shit-thick Taff, but the demented low-IQ grin of the hardened hooligan. I sent word down the train that on my word, everyone was to fucking open the gates of hell, after opening the doors of the train first of course.

'Chelsea!' I roared at the top of my voice, and instantly my roar came back magnified 3,476 times, cause that's how many of us were on that train.

We piled out onto the platform like violence-starved violent people. It was one of the biggest offs I'd ever seen, and I'd seen plenty of offs go off. It was going off everywhere. Fucking great it was an' all. Cause this was what we lived for. Football-related violence. And now the fucking coppers had only given us the best fucking Christmas present in the fucking world.

'Come on, Steve, get stuck in,' shouted Gal.

That snapped me out of my daydream and I made straight for a big ginger cop cunt who was kicking shit out of a couple of Chelsea boys from a Royal Tunbridge Wells firm. A swift kick to the kidneys and the cunt went down like a ton of bricks, or a ton of feathers, whichever is heavier. There then followed a barrage of kicks as we made sure he stayed down.

I turned round and saw Gal being led away by two coppers. Before, it had been a ticking off by the local magistrate – some were in firms themselves – and a bit of community service if you got nicked. Now, I wasn't sure. That's why as they threw Gal into the back of the van I thought, 'Fuck it, let's see what they do to him.' As the doors of the van shut, and Gal's screams and desperate pleadings, sobbings and attempts to self-injure started, I made a mental note to remind myself not to forget to remember to find out what they did to him. Then I turned my attentions back to the ruck of rucks going on around me.

The coppers were now in retreat. Chelsea were everywhere, going at it like deranged baboons on crack. All I could hear was 'Get off me, is it?' and 'Aaaah, is it?' and 'Jesus, he's got a machete, is it?' Gal had even fashioned a sheep out of that shit that passes for stuffing in a British Rail seat and was taunting the Taffs with it, waving it at them going, 'Ooh, wouldn't you like to have sex with me? Ooh, come on, you pervs, stick it in me.' It was so funny, you know, really hilarious, it still makes me laugh now, and feel a bit sick for some reason.

'Right,' I said, 'that's them sorted, time for it to kick off at the kick-off.'

We made our way out of the station, leaving a couple of young firms to finish off the Taff coppers. The young firms were our future and it made me feel proud inside and outside to see them going at it. They were learning, see, and in their case, learning from the best. They hero-worshipped me, had posters of me on their bedroom walls, tattoos of me on their arms, set up fan clubs, that sort of thing. And in return, I took them under my wing, threw them a few scraps from time to time, the odd Scouser here, a Manc there, nothing too tricky. One or two of them could probably have coped with a Millwall cunt or a West Ham slag, but I didn't want any of them getting too big for their DMs, though they probably would do cause most of them were still growing.

After chucking out the regulars, we settled into a pub called The Menstruating Sow, Boyo, near the Swansea ground. Everyone was yabbering away ten to the fucking dozen, recounting tales of the ruck at the station.

'Then three of them grabbed me from behind, but I kicked the first cunt in the head and he went down, then his mate come at me with his fucking truncheon, right, but I fucking ducked under it and chinned the fucker, and the other cunt then bottled it and ran.'

All over the boozer, similar stories were being told. Cause that was part of it an' all, see, the telling. It's like that thing about shagging a fantastic bird like Kate Moss or Denise Van Outen or some other slag. If you couldn't tell your mates about it after, would you do it? No, course you fucking wouldn't, there'd be no point. It was then that Young Gal burst into the boozer looking for me.

'Steve, Steve!' he shouted at the top of his prepubescent unbroken voice.

I'd just been in the middle of recounting how I'd bitten the toes off some copper, or it could have been the ticket inspector, and was none too happy about being interrupted.

'This had better be good,' I said to Young Gal.

'It is, it is,' he squealed. The whole gaff had gone quiet now. If he was taking the piss, he'd be fucking getting it good 'n' properly good 'n' proper.

'Outside!' he shrieked, a good ten octaves higher than I could ever have hoped to have reached. 'They've ringed the pub, fucking millions of them.'

I stood up and went over to the one window that was still unbroken. Sure enough, just as Young Gal had said, outside the pub there were fucking millions of Taff coppers. Only this time there was something different about them. At first, I couldn't place it so I called Steve over, but he was a useless cunt and couldn't suss it either. Neither could Gal, Gal, Gal, Steve, Gal, three geezers from a Shepherd's Bush firm or the weeping landlord of the pub, who I dragged away from the cellar where three of the lads were still giving him a seeing to. Incredibly, it was Young Gal who spotted it.

'They're fucking decked out in full riot gear,' he squeaked.

'Shit me,' I said, 'the little cunt's only right, isn't he?'

I gave him a right fucking slap then, just to make sure it didn't go to his head.

'Let that be a lesson to you,' I said, and then I looked again, and this time I saw it. Fucking millions of them togged up like fucking modern-day gladiators. And we were the lions. Something else bugged me though. That analogy. It didn't quite work. But I didn't have time to think of anything better.

'Right, here's what we'll do,' I said as everyone listened in. 'Let's charge out there and go fucking mental.'

Everyone agreed it was a brilliant plan so I burst out into the miserable Swansea overcast gloom followed by my army of fiercely loyal and dedicated boys, right into one of the biggest rucks in fucking history. If I'd thought the off at the station was a big off, it was nothing compared to this off. This off was one fuck of an off.

But if we'd thought it was going to be easy, and to be fair, I doubt many of us did, we were very wrong. The riot gear turned the cops into fucking terminators (I was happier with that analogy, apart from the bit about them being from the future), and try as we did, we couldn't get at them. That's when I saw a sickening sight. Some of the Chels were running. It tore my heart asunder, spliced it from aorta to aorta, my very soul felt like it had been wrenched from my body.

'Stand and fight,' I screamed, 'stand and fucking fight, Chelsea.'

But we were losing numbers as geezers I'd thought were hard scattered like fucking pussycats. And those that didn't run were being set upon by the Taff riot cops and being kicked to fuck. I ran after some of those that were running – not running myself of course, running after the cunts who had run, that's totally different – grabbed them and threw them back into the fray, shouting, 'We're fucking Chels, we don't run from not no one not so not never, now fucking get back in there and ruck, you cunts.'

It was fucking useless though. We were being made to look like cunts, by Taffs an' all. This wasn't going to look good. And to make matters worse, I was pretty sure I'd seen a reporter from the hooligan daily, *Cunt News*, poncing around the place, sticking his pug-ugly fucking nose in where it wasn't fucking wanted. A few of us managed to make it to the ground for the game, but there were more fucking riot cunts there, so we had no joy and had to watch the fucking football with the fucking Swansea boys taunting us all the time, giving it some with the lip. Course we gave as good as we got, coming back at them with some very clever ripostes such as 'You're gonna get your fucking Taff heads kicked in' and 'Sheep shaggers, sheep shaggers', but it didn't really make us feel any better; made us feel worse in fact, cause sticks and stones can hurt your bones, but words can never harm them, and that's what we wanted to do, harm them badly with sticks and stones and knives and bottles and anything we could lay our hands on. There was one moment when Gal found a brick and lobbed it into the disabled section, splitting some Taff cunt in a wheelchair's head open, but it didn't really help. It was fucking dismal. A bad result and no mistake. Course, we'd had a fucking great time, had two of the best rucks I'd ever been involved in, but we'd come out of it looking bad, looking like muppets, like we'd been taught a lesson. Yeah, there was now another firm in the game, but they were playing by their own rules, only, as it was the same game, that didn't seem fair.

The journey back was full of the usual tales of bravado and the traditional teeth display put on by the younger firms, where they'd parade naked up and down the carriages wearing necklaces made from all the teeth they'd kicked out of Taff cunts. But deep down inside, I knew this was a turning point. Not on the railway tracks, but in my life. After this, I knew things might very well not be the same ever again. Then again, they just might be. The only good thing to come out of the day was the laugh we had when we found out about Gal's sentence. They'd only decided to go and make a fucking example out of the cunt. Seven years in a maximum-security fucking prison, in solitary the whole time with no chance of appeal. Very fucking funny, HM Government, but I'd still be there to give him that kicking when he got out and no fucking mistake.

chapter fucking twelve

In hooligan terms, 1983 was a watershed, though why a shed made of water signifies change is fucking beyond me. Anyway, things were definitely different after that. One of the main differences was that it was 1984. Yeah, 19-fucking-84. According to George Orwell, a prize cunt if ever there was one, we were all meant to be zombies by now and living on a farm in Paris or London or some fucking shit like that. Well, he was one cunt who got his fucking comeuppance, weren't he? He got it so wide of the fucking mark he never wrote another book after that year. Far from being a zombie, I was turning other people into zombies, with my fucking fists. One geezer's still in a coma to this day; I sometimes send him a birthday card when I remember.

I'd spent the summer at the European Championships in France. Even though the England team weren't there, it was another great victory for the English if you know what I mean. I had such a fucking laugh I stayed out there after the tournament. I mean, what could be better than foreign cunts on tap? It was fucking blinding. But come August, I'd had my fill of shoving baguettes up Frog arses and headed home in time for the start of the new season. (Some geezers never made it back, though, and are still there now; like those cunts out in Korea who think the fucking war is still on, they think the fucking European Championships are still going on, wankers.)

Chelsea had narrowly avoided relegation the previous season and so had been promoted, or something like that. Anyway, we were back in the big time and determined to make sure every cunt knew it. And with the Old Bill now getting more involved, it was fucking mint. Some say it was the golden era of hooliganism, a fucking beautiful time that will live on forever in fairy tales of extreme violence. I don't know about that, and frankly, I don't give a blind shit, I just know that I was rucking, fighting, scrapping, kicking, brawling, punching, nutting, slashing and cutting like there was no tomorrow. I was in ruck heaven, which meant for loads of cunts it was unhappy ever after.

But there was also something else, something, very, very else. It's not easy to put into words exactly what the fucker was, but I'll try, otherwise you're not going to know what it is, are you, unless you have my phone number and ring me up, only even then I'm going to have to put it into words to tell you. It was like time was running out. Yeah, that's it. It was like time itself was fucking bottling it, the slag, and legging it away from us. Nobody knew it then really, and no one does now neither, but somehow there was a sense that we had to get as many kickings in as possible cause soon, very soon, in the not too distant near to back then future, it would all be over.

So with that hanging over our heads, even though, as I said, we didn't realise it then and still don't now, I was more than a little surprised when Gal turned to me one day and said, 'You coming to the march this weekend?'

I was that fucking startled I dropped the geezer I was laying into at the time and turned to face Gal, full on, eyelash to eyelash. I didn't know what the fuck the cunt was on about.

'What the fuck are you on about, you cunt?' I said, my thoughts magically transforming themselves into speech.

'The National Front march, down Southall, to get rid of all the Pakis,' he said.

'Get rid of all the Pakis?' I said with a sneer that had 'You're a pathetic little piss stain not worthy of being a piece of shit on my shoe' written all over it. 'What would we want to do that for, you cunt? If they all fuck off, we won't be able to go Paki-bashing any more, will we, and then you'll have deprived me of one of my favourite pastimes, you fucking slag.'

That threw the bastard. I should have been a fucking politician, me.

'Well,' he continued, very much on the back fucking foot now due to the verbal roasting I'd just given him, 'it ain't cos of the Pakis, is it, it's cause it's fucking great for a ruck. Last time we blah blah blah blah blah blah blah blah blah.'

OK, he didn't actually say 'blah blah blah', but he could have done for all I knew. All I heard was that it was great for a ruck, and that was fucking music to my ears; Chopin, I think it sounded like. Being the ruck addict I was, I was always on the look out for new, fresh, uncut, pure, unadulterated, grade-A rucks. That's why, the following Sunday, I found myself walking down Southall High Street holding a banner which read 'Keep England' and, on the other side, 'White'. Not on me own, like, you understand, with about 300 others and 500 police who were there to protect us. Yeah, figure that one out. The Old Bill were only there to look after us cunts. As I strode down the street, I had a grin on me mush as wide as a basket of chipmunks.

It was not unlike running with the England cause a lot of the lads there were from other firms and, as I've made clear, normally I'd've fucking seen to them good 'n' proper. They knew that and I knew that, there was a mutual knowing, if you like. But in this case, we were one firm, united by far-right fascistic ideology. Course, a lot of the firms were Chels cause Chelsea were a proudly racist club back then, founding members of the Kick Racism Into Football movement, in fact.

The difference was the Old Bill. Unlike when we went away with Chelsea or England, or just went away, when the Old Bill were there to try and stop us having it out with whoever the fuck we were playing's firm, this time the Old Bill were there to uphold our demo-fucking-cratic right to express our politi-fucking-cal opinions. And Jesus, didn't the cunts hate it. Not cause of having to stop us laying into the Pakis. Cause of wanting to be *with* us instead of around us, see? Cause they all hated Pakis too then, a lot of them still do today, actually, and what they really wanted was to tear into the cunts themselves. But they couldn't, could they? They had to wait till they got the cunts back to their stations or their vans for that. That's fucking politics for you.

'Fucking hell, Gal,' I said to Gal after we'd been marching for about 40 seconds. 'We've been marching for 40 seconds and there's no sign of it going off yet. Were you fucking having a laugh with me?'

'No, mate,' said Gal. And somehow I knew he was telling the truth. But I chose to fucking let him have it anyway.

'Oi, didn't your old girl used to buy her fags off that Paki geezer in the newsagent?' I said to him with, I felt, just the right level of menace in my voice.

He didn't have to say anything. He knew the game was up.

I puffed my chest out like a sackful of Puffa Puffa Rice. 'Lads,' I said, my fingers Pavlovianly curling up into a fist, 'I think we got ourselves a Paki here.'

The cunt only tried to make a run for it, didn't he? That marked him out as a Paki if nothing else. Well, he had it coming to him, leaving the other 299 of us with no option but to pile into him. (It would have been 799, but, as I've said, the Old Bill had to leave off.)

So we'd had an off, but it was just an appetiser, an hors d'oeuvre before the main course, for which I was intent on having the ruck du jour, which was one almighty fucking ruck. Fortunately, I didn't have to wait too long for it, otherwise the imagined waiter in this set-up would've had his fucking head kicked in and no fucking error.

As we rounded a corner, I heard an unmistakable sound, at least to me. Some of the lads thought it was the mating cry of the short-horned lesser-breasted bullfinch, but I knew better. It was the low rumble of the violence-intent mob; easy to confuse with the mating cry of the short-horned lesser-breasted bullfinch, I grant you, but to my refined ear palate, highly distinct.

My whole body clenched itself, ready for ruck action. I was a UXB and I wasn't about to be defused. I saw them first as we rounded another corner: a baying, seething, swaying mob of woolly, left-wing, whinging

Anti Nazi League poofs. As we neared them, the jeering and taunting reached fever pitch.

'Fucking fascist cunts,' shouted one cunt.

'Nazi wankers,' shouted another.

'NF bastards,' screamed yet another.

It was all fairly accurate stuff, but it incensed me ever more nonetheless. From within the confines of my jacket, I fondled my secret weapon, a weapon specifically designed to be a ruck catalyst. I pulled the brick out slowly, kissed it for good luck and hurled it into the centre of the trendy lefty horde.

It caught an ugly fucker smack in the middle of his pug-ugly face. Claret instantly started pouring down his really-not-very-good-looking visage. It was fucking lovely, and part of me wished that he was a haemophiliac and it would never end.

In response, a shower of bricks, bottles and jelly babies rained down upon us. The police line was stretched to bursting. To regain some tautness, they went concentric and formed two encircling circles to hem us in, but it was too late; a big skinhead from Knebworth, his ear fashioned into a swastika, had breached the police line and was laying into the Billy Bragg-loving slags.

'*Sieg heil, Sieg heil,*' chanted Steve next to me.

'Oi, is that fucking foreign lingo, you cunt?' I said to him.

'Yeah, but it's OK—'

That was as far as he got. He'd gone so far out of line

I had no choice. I cut up the cunt good 'n' proper, leaving him lying on the floor in a right mess, with the traditional Chelsea Foxhunters calling card stuck in his eye. Then I turned my attentions to the socialist scumbags.

By now, the police line had dissolved like dissolvable stitches, the type Steve would probably need, though I don't think they'd been invented by then. It was a fucking free-for-all, lefty cunts going down left, right and left of centre. I tell you, it was a good job that the Labour-Party, union-activist cunts were wearing Anti Nazi League badges and we were wearing anti-Anti Nazi League badges, otherwise I could well have been lamping my own, which, truth be told, wouldn't have bothered me all that much.

After about ten minutes or so, I took my customary breather. I liked to look around and survey the scene, watch my minions, if you like, so that afterwards I could give them tips and, where necessary, praise or beatings. To the left of me, Gal, Steve and Gal were pummelling a couple of black bastards. To the right of me, Steve, Gal and Steve were cutting up some Yid slag. I turned round to check out what was going on behind me. In amidst the Dante's Infernoesque scene of human depravity was the most beautiful sight I had ever seen.

Laying into some Red-Ken cunt like a sex-starved, food-starved, undernourished tiger on heat was the most fantastic bird I had ever seen. She was really fucking letting him have it and of course, what with her being a bird and that, he couldn't fucking hit her back or nothing, could he? (Unless she'd been his missus, which she wasn't.) What's more, apart from the clothes she was wearing, she was stark bollock naked.

As a violent thug, I'd come across women before, but they were all slags, tarts, slappers and dogs, good for one thing and one thing only. This bird was different. I was drawn to her for other reasons, not just cause I wanted to fuck her up the arse and come on her tits, though I wanted to do that as well of course.

It was like a light had been switched on in my brain, and not just a single, solitary bulb glowing dimly. This was a fuck-off huge great neon fucker, the sort of thing God probably used when he said, 'Let there be light.'

As I watched her deliver blow after blow after blow to the head of the commie cunt lying brain-dead on the floor beneath her, my heart melted. I knew that I was destined not so much to spend the rest of my life with her but to marry her, have a couple kids and then fuck off for the rest of my life. I strode over to the Russki bastard she'd been seeing to.

As I was a top boy, the sea of NF surrounding him parted to let me through. With a quick glance to make sure she was watching, I cradled the geezer's head in my hand and then nutted him over and over and over and over again until the cracked shell of his head was spewn all over the floor. It made for an impressive sight and I'd challenge any bird not to fancy the fucking pants off me after that. It certainly did the trick for her. Within moments, we were fucking like frenzied ferrets whilst simultaneously inflicting considerable damage on the Trotskyite bastards around us. Sex and violence, violence and sex: whichever way you looked at it, it was fucking great.

Two weeks later, at Cricklewood Registry Office, we were hitched. Our families hated each other on sight, which made for an almighty ruck at the wedding, it was fucking fantastic. Looking at my wife belt some cunt of a cousin of mine in her bloodstained wedding dress is a picture I'll carry around with me for ever, in my head I mean. I haven't got any actual pictures of the wedding, as the photographer looked at my bird so I did him and then he fucked off out of it.

For the honeymoon, I booked a real treat: Manchester United away. We travelled up from London together in the bridal carriage of the footy special. The lads had done it up a fucking treat and even thrown in a few Millwall for us to kick shit out of on the way up.

Arriving at Manchester Piccadilly it was obvious that the Manc wanks had got word of my nuptials. As we alighted on to the platform, a mob of them came charging at us, chucking great lumps of rock-hard confetti as they did so. Course, the Old Bill were there in numbers, too. It made for one fuck of a wedding present; the missus fucking loved it and had the time of her life kicking the almighty crap out of all and sundry with the 2,500-hole cement-toecapped DM high heels Gal, Gal, Gal, Gal and Steve had given her.

The rest of the honeymoon passed in a blur of kickings, kickings, sex and more kickings, it was the perfect start to married life. Violence was the glue in our relationship and as long as we had that, nothing would ever split us up. Unfortunately, no one told that to some Scouse cunts in Belgium, so what I thought was the end of the middle of the beginning, was in fact the beginning of the middle of the end of the beginning.

chapter fucking unlucky for some cunt thirteen

I'll tell you something, this writing lark's a fucking doddle. I mean, look at me. Well don't, otherwise I'll kick your fucking teeth in, but here I am at 11.30 in the morning sitting in The Fucking Fucking Cunting Shithole and Cheese Omelette, a pint by my side, a fag in me gob and plenty of sad, unemployed cunts to beat up when I fancy it, and all I've got to do is think about my life and write the fucker down. And some cunt's only paying me to do it. If that's not taking the absolute fucking piss, I don't know what is taking the absolute fucking piss. I mean, I can write what the fuck I like, look: arse, bollocks, shit, fuck, arse again, cunt, twat, turd. See? Fucking magic.

I just reread that last chapter and, frankly, it's fucking brilliant, the best yet. As I reread, I relived all those kickings and rucks, and not just in my head. I did some serious brain damage to the barman reading that bit about meeting the wife. He wasn't happy, but he's a mate, so fuck him. But it did occur to me that while I was getting all hi-fucking-falutin with all that politics, I was forgetting about football. I mean, fair dos, at the time, going on an NF march and going to a football match were practically the same thing, but to the more cultured hooligan eye, there were differences. At football we used to throw bananas at black *players* and make monkey noises, but on a march we'd throw bananas at black *people* and make monkey noises. There were other differences as well, such as the type of monkey noises and the country of origin of the bananas, but, fundamentally, what I'm saying is let's get back to the fucking football.

So, marriage. Me and the wife were together for two weeks. Yeah, I fucking know it's meant to be for life, but, I'll tell you, it felt like a fucking lifetime. Jesus did she fucking change. She only fucking wanted to see me twice a week. I mean, that's the first fucking step on the road to cuntdom. Next thing, she'd be wanting to fucking move in. But that wasn't the worst thing. After we'd got hitched, I only fucking found out she was West Ham, didn't I? Yeah, West Ham. West fucking Ham. The Ham of the fucking West.

We were home to those East London cunts after our

honeymoon game up at United. I was fucking looking forward to it. It was going to be like a second honeymoon. As per, I met up with the boys in The You're A Fucking Cunt and Aga.

'The wife coming today, Steve?' said Gal.

'Course she fucking is, you cunt, she wouldn't fucking miss this one for nothing. We're going to give those cunts a going over they won't fucking forget in a hurry and renew our vows at the same fucking time,' I said.

'Nice one,' said Gal.

'Yeah, nice one,' said Steve.

'Like it,' said Gal.

'Yeah, like it,' said Gal.

'Nice one,' said Gal again.

'Yeah, the fucking vicar's booked to be in the middle of the North Stand at 3.30, so it's got to fucking go off before that. I want it all to be perfect for my little lady, no one fucks up, right?'

'Right,' said Gal, Gal, Gal, Gal, Gal, Steve, Steve, Gal, Steve, Gal and Gal all together.

'Right,' said Steve on his own.

Yeah, I knew I was fucking spoiling her, which can be a big mistake with birds, but I was in love, weren't I, I weren't thinking straight. Some cunt once said treat 'em mean, keep 'em keen. Well, my philosophy had always been fucking smack 'em one and they'll know who's boss; kind of the same thing but more overtly violent. So on this occasion I wasn't sticking to my own philoso-fucking-phy and fuck me, was I going to pay for it.

We left the boozer well tanked up and headed for the ground. It was still early, about 12.47, but we'd got word that West Ham's notorious International Monetary Fund, or IMF, were drinking in The Big Fat Poof Queer Hairy Bumhole and Esther Rantzen, so we set off to introduce those cunts to pre-match entertainment, Chelsea style.

As we marched down the Fulham Road, I could tell the lads were fucking up for it. They were that excited there was some pushing and jostling. Now pushing, that's fair game, but jostling – well, that is slap bang wallop what a picture, what a photograph, stick it in the family, stick it in the family, stick it in the family album well out of order. It's fucking inexcusable in a lowly firm of cunts from Doncaster. In Chelsea's top firm, it's fucking, fucking, fucking inexcusable. So I had a word, didn't I? That sorted it and by the time the boozer came into view, all indiscipline had been eradicated.

'Fuck me, what a stench, I can smell those cunts from here,' I said, sniffing.

And truth be told, I could. Christ, did they hum with their Aramis City-gent aftershave and their eau de cockle-and-mussel inbuilt niff, the niff that emanates from all those wankers cause they're born within the pong of Bow Bells market. Some of the lads started coughing, it was so bad. And then retching and bringing up great thick green gobs of goo. That's when I had an idea.

'Oi,' I bellowed above the guttural Arabic type din. 'Any cunt who flobs fucking gets it, right? Bring it up, but don't let it out. We're saving it for those cunts in there.' I gestured towards the pub.

A massive grin went round the lads, like a Mexican wave-grin. They knew what I meant and therefore, using what basic logic they had, knew what it meant for those West Ham wankers drinking in that boozer.

With our mouths primed and full to the brim with mucusy green mucus and in some cases, mucusy yellow mucus and in the case of still others who had brought up some blood, mucusy reddy green mucus, we approached the pub.

On my command – not easy with a mouth as full as mine – we burst in, our ammo at the ready.

As one, the West Ham turned to face us. For a twillisecond, time stood still. As I've said already, it's an incredible moment, that moment just before it kicks off. If I could bottle it and sell it on eBay I'd probably have enough for a portable DVD player by now; but I never fucking bottle it, so that isn't going to happen.

Then, like a swarm of bees or flock of birds or shoal of fish or any other large group of animals that is actually made up of individuals, but moves as one, they moved, as one, towards us. But instead of giving another command to fucking let them have it, I waited. I'd seen *Zulu*, I'd seen Michael twatting Caine tell those cunting soldiers of his to wait until they could see the whites of the Zulus' eyes before firing, as opposed to the blacks of their skins which any fucker could see from miles away. So I waited. And waited and waited and waited. Until the West Ham were almost on us. Then, spilling some of the amassed mucal bullet in me gob, gave the word.

Instantly a wall of predominantly green, but with the odd bit of yellow and red speckled throughout, emerged from our combined mouth, the same combined mouth that had done that Mexican-wave grin earlier. It was a fucking beautiful sight, a tsunami of phlegm. It hit the West Ham cunts full on, covering them from head to toe. They'd been green to charge us like they had, now they really were green, a ha ha ha ha ha ha ha ha ha ha ha ha ha ha ha ha.

Under the hail of halitosis-fuelled gob, they retreated back to the far end of the pub. We fucking pissed ourselves. They looked a right sorry sight. West Ham's famous IMF fucking made to look like fucking saps. Yeah, it was a top moment, but I knew better than to savour it for too long. Though they're cunts, I'll say this about West Ham: they're hard cunts and one thing they do not like is being covered in highly contagious thick green sputum. They weren't about to scuttle back to their east London shitholes. And as if to prove me right, back then and now, like a slimy green monster emerging from a swamp, they regrouped and started back towards us.

Gal, Gal and Gal started desperately coughing again in an attempt to reload their gobs.

'Leave it, lads. This time we're going to hit them with these,' I said, and as if to illustrate my point, I raised my fists.

The lads got the point and stopped coughing, apart from Gal who had bronchitis.

We all knew what was going to happen next. As the West Ham approached, the mound of green jelly split into two and their top boy emerged from within, walking straight towards me. It was like a well-rehearsed dance, a way of doing things that stretched back maybe ten years, to the beginning of the modern hooligan era, the cunteolithic period. And fuck me, did he look a picture. If anything, he'd taken the brunt of our gob hits and was fucking caked in the stuff. Fair play to the cunt, though, he must have known what he looked like, but he kept on coming, till we was just inches apart, eyeballing each other. Then he wiped away most of the gob from his face and I got the biggest cunting surprise of my cunting life. Not only was the cunt not a he but a she, he was also only my fucking wife. That hit harder than any crowbar to the back of the head.

'What the fuck are you doing here?' I managed to utter. And then, 'And why are you fucking pretending to be the IMF's top fucking boy?' Both pertinent questions I felt.

The reply was curt in the extreme.

'I am the IMF's top boy, you cunt.'

Well, that was fucking it. A red pea-souper descended

145

and we went at it like kingdom fucking coming great huge truckloads of salty white cum come. And so did everyone else. It was fucking mayhem. Course, the Old Bill turned up and spoilt it all by carting a load of us off to the nick, but by then it was too late; my marriage was as good as dead and buried. We tried Relate to patch things up, but after we'd kicked shit out of 14 of their top boy counsellors, we called it a day. I mean, it was never going to fucking work out, was it? What with her being West Ham and me being Chels. I suppose I should have fucking found out before marrying her, but that would have meant actually talking to her, and I wasn't big on that.

And then to cap it all, it only turned out she was fucking pregnant, didn't it? If that wasn't the icing on the cake, I don't know what fucking was. I mean what self-respecting hard cunt is going to stick around when there're kids involved?

So that was that for my marriage. I still saw the wife, or ex-wife, every time Chelsea played West Ham. It was heartbreaking, literally. Every time we ran in to each other we used to go at it hammer, nail and tongs, trying to rip the other's heart out and snap it in two. Neither of us succeeded and I like to think that over the years, it was a draw, which I just won.

As for her being pregnant, she had the kid, a boy. Or girl. I got access every third weekend and for a week every summer, but told them where they could stick that.

'You know where you can stick that,' I said.

And they did.

The whole sorry episode was good for one thing and one thing only: it taught me that no one was ever going to come between me and Chels. I was married to them, for better or worse, in sickness and in health, till death do us part. A-fucking-men.

chapter fucking fourteen

On the last day of the 1987–88 season, Chelsea were in dire fucking danger of being relegated. According to the 'fans', they'd been fucking shite on the pitch, something I'd completely fucking missed cause of all the punch-ups I'd been having off the pitch and, on one or two occasions, on it. That's the thing about being a top boy, you've got to give it 100 fucking per cent. You've got to be totally focused on the beating in hand. If not, you're history. And a cunt. I knew an ex-former-one-time top boy who ran with Everton, Gal, I think his name was. He got fucking cocky, didn't he? Started kicking some cunt in and watching the game as well. Next thing he knows, the cunt he was kicking in is making *him* look like a cunt by kicking him in. Stupid cunt.

There was also another reason why I didn't let my mind wander whilst administering a fucking mental shit-kicking to all the cunts I administered shit-kickings to – a reason I alluded to earlier, but if you're too fucking thick to remember or can't be fucking bothered to read it again, I'll tell you. I said time felt like it was running out. And due to that massive off in Belgium, which I've also mentioned before, and one or two other offs closer to home, time now felt like it was fucking scarpering double-quick-time pronto with its fucking tail between its legs. (There, I've fucking saved you the trouble of having to read over what I fucking wrote before, you fucking owe me.)

The fucking authori-fucking-ties were going fucking mental saying something's got to be done about the hooligan problem. Now every time it went off big time, it was like giving them more fucking ammu-fucking-nition to say something's got be done about the hooligan problem, and say it more times and louder.

As far as I was concerned, if they had a fucking problem, they should have fucking come down and had it out with me, fucking stated their point of view and then let me state mine, with my fists, in their face. End of problem, you get me? But no, those sort of cunts operate on a different level, don't they? They fucking mouth off, with their mouths, let their mouths do the talking if you will. It fucks me off big time now and it fucked me off big time then. I do my talking with my fists and feet and forehead and knife and sledgehammer and crowbar, and I make a fuckload more sense than those cunts. But we was lumbered and that was that.

You see, the way I looked at it, there was no hooligan problem; in fact, the whole fucking hooligan thing was the answer to a problem in the first place. Geezers are always going to want a fucking punch-up, so what better place to fucking do it than at fucking football? (And in the pub, at weddings, nightclubs, when some cunt looks at you etc. etc., see earlier, you cunts, I'm not writing that again.) It's fucking perfect. The sides are set, you hate them, they hate you, you fucking go for it, end of. Or in some cases, you then go for it again later outside the ground and then at the station still later and then walking back from the station if you find some stragglers. The point is, it works, and everybody's happy, apart from the cunts who get the living fucking shit beaten out of them, but they're cunts so they can fuck off.

So it was important that when I was rucking I didn't let my mind drift onto anything other than matters pertaining to the ruck, which meant when one of these 'fans' came up to me with a request, I had no fucking idea what the cunt was on about.

'Listen, Steve, we need your help,' he said.

'Who the fuck are you and who the fuck do you think you are coming into my boozer and asking for my help? There'd better be a fucking good reason for this, mate, otherwise you are going to be fucking sorry.'

'But I'm Chels,' he said.

'Chels? Are you having a fucking laugh?' I said, standing up and pushing the chair I'd been sitting on back so that its legs scraped against the floor with that familiar and unmistakable 'it's about to go off' sound.

'Look,' said the fan, his voice going up by about eight octaves so he sounded even more of a fucking girl poof cunt than he already was, 'I'm a season ticket holder.'

He thrust a tatty-looking booklet at me. In the heat of the moment, I thought he was going for his tool and, being a confirmed devotee of the fucking belt the absolute cunting fuck out of them first and ask questions later (assuming they're still conscious and can talk) school of philoso-fucking-phy, I let him have it, tore into him like a deranged wildcat crack whore on ketamine.

'Err err err err err I'm dying,' said the fan as he lay in a pool of his blood, a pool which was rapidly turning into a lake due to the additional blood he was coughing up.

Now, normally at this juncture, the paramedics would have turned up and taken him away, the Old Bill would have asked a few questions, to which the answer from anyone who didn't want to end up like that cunt would be 'He slipped on a soggy beermat' and that would have been the end of it. But, as I'm sure you've realised having read this far, I'm a decent bloke, and the geezer had asked for me help. He'd taken his beating and if he knew what was good for him, he wouldn't stray out of line again in a hurry. So, out of the kindness of my cunting hooligan heart, I made sure the paramedics were held back and he couldn't be treated until I'd heard what he wanted.

It took a while and a couple more slaps for him to get to the fucking point, but the long and short of the cunt was this: Chelsea needed to win their last game, otherwise they'd be going down, and this 'fan' wanted our help to ensure they did – win their last game that is, not go down. (There was also some other bollocks about play-offs and second legs, but I shut the cunt up before he could get into all that, otherwise he'd have been the one looking for a fucking second leg.)

It was a big fucking ask from one of those cunts who were intent on ruining it for the rest of us, but, frankly, I was touched by his belief that if me and the boys played for Chelsea they would win.

'We'll fucking do it, mate. With us playing for Chelsea, whoever the fuck they're playing won't have a fucking chance. You sort it and we'll be there.'

Personally, I thought I'd made a fucking mag-fucking-nanimous fucking gesture, but for some reason the cunt looked at me like I'd just spoken to him in some wog language.

'No, you don't understand,' he said.

And then, very, very quickly as that unmistakable chair-leg-scraping-on-floor sound unmistakably reappeared, 'We don't want you to play for Chelsea, we want you to sort out the other team so that they can't beat us.'

Having made the sound which cannot be mistaken, it seemed a shame to waste it, so I kicked him in the teeth and gave him a slap anyway, but I stopped short of giving him a complete fucking going over again. And before you think for one fucking cunting wankisecond that that was because I fucking bottled it, let me put you bang to rights straight away. The reason was this: in all my time following football there was one thing I'd never done – twat a player. And that fucking got me, gnawed away at my innards like a fucking parasitic cunt. I mean, who the fuck did those footballers think they were? They fucking ran around the pitch and kicked the ball about or something and that gave them the right not to be slapped by the likes of me? Do what? Is someone having a laugh or is someone having a laugh?

Being handed to me on a plate, albeit by a fan cunt, was an opportunity to do away with that gnawing pain before it turned into an ulcer or cancer or gout, and by fuckadee Christ al-cunting-mighty, it was an opportunity I was going to grab with both hands and then fucking headbutt into next Wednesday week, maybe even Thursday.

'Gal, get this cunt a drink,' I said.

Gal looked the cunt up and down with the sort of disdain he normally reserved for taxidermists. We all knew what was going to happen next. Being the joker he is, Gal only didn't get the cunt a drink, didn't he not? No. He only nicked the cunt's wallet and got us all a drink, and a cigar, packet of fags, packet of pork scratchings and a commemorative tankard each. Made no odds to me.

'You've come to the right geezer, mate,' I said to the fan, masticated pork scratchings spraying all over him as I spoke. 'Now, tell us exactly where and when, and, unless you want to get twatted again, while telling us don't look at anyone or anyone's bird, don't spill anyone's pint or call anyone a cunt. And don't be a Yid or a Paki.'

Well, he was new to the game, I felt it was only fair to give him a few tips. What he said was that the team Chelsea were playing that day – Middlesbrough, coincidentally also the team whose firms we were going to have it out with later on – would arrive by coach *before* the start of the game, and then they'd go into some changing-rooms, also before the start of the game, to change into their strip. Then, just before the start of the game, they'd leave the changing-rooms and go out onto the pitch where, right at the very start of the game, they'd start the game. I tell you, it was like another fucking world, and a right cunt's world at that, but, in terms of helping me get rid of that gnaw in my duodenum (or possibly ileum), it was important information, so I listened like a fucking elephant-eared bat with one of those old-fashioned ear trumpets.

I was grateful to the fan cunt for what he told us, but unfortunately, as he was telling us, Steve's bird came in, and his eyes glanced in her direction for 0.000000000000000001 of a second. It was a stupid mistake to make, but not wholly unexpected from someone so wet behind the ears in terms of hooliganism, and in terms of the blood pouring from a gaping head wound. As the lads went to town on him, I sat back to plan my strategy.

After 15 more pints, I'd boiled it down to this: we had to get into the changing-rooms and kick shit out of the Middlesbrough players.

It was neat, it was compact, but most importantly, it worked. It was fucking watertight.

We left the pub in a state of high excitement. Apart from anything else, there was another ruck on the day's agenda, an agenda which was already pretty ruck-heavy and essentially read: item 1, ruck; item 2, ruck; item 3, ruck; item 4, ruck; item 5, ruck; and item 6, any other business. So we were happy. Walking down the King's Road, we sang a few old hooligan spirituals and tap-danced. We were men, bonding, in a non-homosexual way with no chance of catching AIDS, even though it didn't really exist then. Or maybe it had just started or something, but I wouldn't know cause I'm not a poof.

You see, that was what I lived for: violence and the prospect of violence. The rush is like no other. I've never understood people who've never understood people like me. What is there not to like? How can anyone not gain immense pleasure from inflicting serious damage on some cunt? And that afternoon, I was going to serve myself a supersize double fucking helping of pure pleasure.

We made our way to where the fan cunt had told us the Middlesbrough team coach would arrive. It was by a door marked 'Players' Entrance', a door I knew we would have to get through at least twice, though going in opposite directions each time.

A lot of other 'fans' were milling around. They seemed excited as well, but seeing as they weren't about to kick someone's teeth in, I couldn't for the life of me work out why. We did our best to make sure we were incon-fucking-spicuous. It wasn't fucking easy. We stood out like a bunch of sore thumbs in a bucket of mangetouts. When you're used to strutting your stuff and fucking making sure every cunt knows who's boss, it's difficult to not strut your stuff and make sure every cunt doesn't know who's boss. But it was a means, weren't it, to an end. An end of the world for those fucking Middlesbrough players. So we kept it cool.

After about three minutes and seventeen seconds, we got word that the Middlesbrough team coach was about five minutes and eight seconds away. That meant I had five minutes and eight seconds to work out how we were going to get into the changing-rooms. I didn't reckon it would be that tricky. Two security men and a couple of coppers were stood by the players' entrance. Not a massive crew and, on the surface of it, hardly a match for Chelsea's top firm. But complacency is the mother of fermentation, and I for one, and Gal, Steve, Steve and Gal for four more, wasn't going to take any chances. The thought of missing out on the opportunity to teach the players who was boss was almost too much for my large/small intestines to take. It was as if I could feel the pus build-up happening and the septic ulcer forming. If for no other reason than for my personal health and well-being, we had to get in there and kick the unadulterated cunting shit out of those cunts.

'Steve,' I said to Gal.

'Gal,' Gal corrected.

'Yeah, right, Gal. That fucking security guard just looked at you and then he told his mate that he'd slept with your mother for money and she ended up paying him.'

Well, that was like unfurling an enormous and deep-deep-red rag which was more like a king-size duvet cover in front of a bull who had been conditioned using basic Skinnerian behavioural techniques to react very, very badly to the colour red. Gal fucking stormed up to the security guard cunt and offered him out there and then.

Now, I'd chosen Gal because he was no pushover. Course, I could have him – but then I could have anyone – but Gal could handle himself. He'd taken out many a cunt who you'd have expected to have taken him out, so by sending him off to sort out the security guard cunt I was testing the water. You see, any cunt can wear a uniform and look hard. Not wearing a uniform and looking hard, now that's a different story.

It was all over in a matter of seconds and I'd learnt an important lesson: this water was definitely hard water, and I don't mean the sort that those Northern cunts keep banging on about cause it makes a fucking better cup of tea. The security guard had gratefully accepted Gal's offer of an out and with one punch to the head and a knee in the groin as he went down, Gal was toast. Fluff. Mung dust. Beeswax. Dobbin fuel. Anal horsehair.

The other lads clocked it too and I could sense a ripple of unease rippling through them. A ripple that, if left untethered, could become a gentle lapping, then a small wave, then before you knew it a giant fucking monster of a wave, the sort that surfers love.

'Gal,' I said to Gal.

'Yes,' said Gal.

'Go and get Gal and stand him up against the wall. Put the fingers of both his hands in the V-sign position, and then, on my signal, make him give the V-sign to the security guard.'

Gal raced over to where Gal lay. At last, his City and Guilds in basic puppetry was going to come in useful. I gave him the nod and, with all the skill of a puppet grandmaster, he made Gal come to life and flick the security guard the V. It had the desired effect. The ripple smoothed out. In the eyes and minds of the lads, Gal had had the last laugh and shown the security guard who was boss. It was an important victory on the mental battlefield, but if we were to win this war, we'd have to win the physical battle as well; after all, it wasn't an alien race consisting solely of consciousness and having no physical presence that we were taking on.

The Middlesbrough team coach was now two minutes and fifty-seven seconds away and unlike in certain cartoons and films where somehow they can make a short space of time last a lot longer, that was all the time I had. I was facing a big challenge, possibly the biggest challenge of my life. Part of me was licking my lips at the prospect, while part of me was in a quandary. Then, as so often happens, help came in the form of something unexpected happening.

We were just close enough to the security guards to pick up the odd scrap of conversation between them.

The one who'd seen to Gal turned to the other one and said, 'I think . . . to be . . . good . . . if . . . out Stan.'

I'd only ever known one geezer called Stan; his old man had had a stall selling third-hand Brillo pads down Neasden market of a Sunday. When I was a kid, me and me mates used to hang around the stall and nick the pads when his old man weren't looking, then sell them down the road for half the price. It was a great scam because technically they were now fourth-hand Brillo pads, but even at half the price that Stan's old man was knocking them out at, we were getting near enough to third-hand prices for them.

The thing was, I remembered going to this Stan's sixth birthday party. Well, I wasn't likely to forget. Did a six spell in junior borstal after it didn't I? Crawled up his old girl's skirt and set fire to her pubes, got charged with being a pubic nuisance, which was reduced on appeal to arson near an arse. But none of that was important right now. What was important was the date of Stan's birthday, 6 May. If I was right, and it wasn't really that big an if, but if I was, the date was none other than 6 May. And, if Stan the security guard was in fact the Stan I used to know, a bigger if, then, putting two and two together, it was Stan's birthday.

The revelation hit me like a thunderbolt wearing knuckledusters – if it had been anything other than an abstract concept, I would have fucking hit the cunt back, twice as fucking hard.

'Steve,' I said.

'Yes, Steve,' said Steve.

'You've got just under two minutes and twelve seconds to get a birthday cake with twenty-five candles and the words 'Happy Birthday Stan' written on it. Fucking sort it.'

Steve took Steve with him and they fucking legged it. The next two minutes felt like the second-longest two minutes of my life, but in reality were probably the fifth-longest two minutes of my life. Sweat started to pour down my back and drip into the cleft of my buttocks and then down into my arse cavity. I chewed my fingernails down to the bone and then chewed the bone down to the bone marrow and the bone marrow down to the hip bone and the hip bone down to the thigh bone and the thigh bone down to the knee bone. I Graeco-Roman wrestled with inner demons and started to self-injure, carving 'Fucking hurry up, Steve' on my arm with a blunt razor-blade. (That's a fuck of a lot to happen in two minutes, no wonder it felt so long.)

Then, just as I was about to chisel 'Jesus, Steve, where the fuck are you?' into my other arm, I saw a dim but definite, throbbing glow in the distance. As it came nearer, that germ of joy that it might be Steve and the cake multiplied into an epidemic of happiness.

'Get in, you fucking lovely cunt,' I shouted as the very definite shape and form of a Madeira sponge cake came into view, followed by the equally definite shape and form of a luxury coach.

Steve was fucking beating the coach hands down, he was the fucking Olym-fucking-pic torchbearer and he was about to enter the fucking stadium.

As he approached, I whipped out a book of logarithm tables and did a very quick time-space calculation. It was crucial that I began the singing of 'Happy Birthday' at exactly the right moment. Of course, it was also crucial that this Stan was the same Stan and thus that it was his birthday, but that cruciality didn't seem to impinge on my thoughts – it just had to be right.

As Steve passed by a point exactly four metres and eight-tenths of a centimetre from the players' entrance, I began singing.

The rest of the lads instantly joined in, as did the fans. Being a complete twat, Steve ran right up to me with the cake, as if my fucking name was Stan and it was my birthday, for fuck's sake; but without disrupting his run, I managed to ease him round to face Stan and, with a slight push, send him off in that direction.

Stan could see Steve approaching him and hear the singing. It was now or never. I could see the Middlesbrough coach pulling up at the door. We moved closer to Stan, our voices booming out the funny versions of 'Happy Birthday' such as the one that ends in 'You look like a monkey and you live in a zoo' and the one that ends in 'You are a fucking wanker and also a cunt too'.

I looked through the crowd at Stan's face. It was a mixture of confusion, joy, anger, delight, jealousy, sloth, uncertainty, certainty, insecurity, security, ambiguosity and unambiguosity. Then, in one gorgeous fucking fell swoop, it all merged into one and, with poof tears in his eyes, he said, 'How, how did you know?'

That was our cue. As the Middlesbrough players disembarked from the coach, we were able to get in amongst them and, still singing 'Happy Birthday', now the funeral march version – 'people die every day', that one – we ducked in through the players' entrance.

It had all worked out fucking lovely and as Stan shouted, 'Who wants a slice?' we made our way towards the changing-room.

As far as I was concerned, that was it; the difficult bit was over and now it was time for some fun. But I was wrong.

I'd been expecting to follow the Middlesbrough players into the changing-room, shut the door behind us and commence the party. That was the plan I'd planned. But I only hadn't fucking counted on there being loads of other cunts there as well, had I? Mingling about with us and the Middlesbrough players was press, hangers-on, refs, mates, physios, birds. Fucking everyone and their fucking mother was in there. It was a mingler's paradise and no mistake, and within moments, maybe even seconds, the Middlesbrough players had blended in and were no more recognisable than any of the other cunts. In effect, we'd lost them.

It was a problem, right enough, but to make matters worse, inside the players' entrance were two changing-rooms; above one was the word 'Home', above the other was the word 'Away'. There was no fucking sign of a Middlesbrough changing-room. Now our problem had doubled. Or squared, depending on whether problems increase linearly or exponentially.

'Steve,' Steve said to me.

'Yeah, what?' I said to Steve.

'There are two changing-rooms. Above one is the word "Home" and above the other is the word "Away". There's no fucking sign of a Middlesbrough changing-room. What the fuck are we going to do?'

It was a good question, and one I'd been pondering myself.

'What the fuck are you fucking on about, Steve?'

It was Gal piping up.

'Steve's the fucking top boy, he knows what to fucking do. You're fucking out of line asking him.'

That was Gal all over, always the loyal lapdog yes-man lieutenant, but Steve didn't take kindly to being called a cunt, in a manner of speaking.

'You what?' he said to Gal.

'You fucking heard, you cunt,' said Gal, calling him a cunt in a more direct way of speaking.

'Come on, then,' said Steve.

I could see where this was going. I'd been in the same or similar situations enough times to know; they were about to start laying into each other. Not a problem normally, but under the present circum-fucking-stances, which were not normal circum-fucking-stances, I reckoned it could be a problem.

'Leave it,' I said to them, 'you can fucking sort it later.'

'But the cunt called me a cunt,' said Steve, clearly put out.

'Well, you are a fucking cunt,' I said to the cunt, 'now fucking leave it.'

But Steve wasn't about to leave it. He was in a right fucking state and next thing you know, he'd fucking stuck one on Gal, a move that was about as bang out of order as you can get because Gal being Gal only didn't fucking turn the other fucking cheek, did he? He fucking went for Steve.

It was a fucking mutiny in the ranks and one that I wasn't fucking going to stand for. But just as I was about to wade in and teach those pair of cunts a fucking lesson, a fucking double maths lesson at that, I had a brain-fucking-wave.

'Oi, Middlesbrough,' I shouted, 'There's a Chelsea cunt here having a go at one of your lot.'

I tell you what, it was only the brain-wave to end all fucking brain-waves. Before you knew it, the Middlesbrough players were piling into Gal, or Steve, they didn't fucking know who was fucking who, did they? And that meant I now knew who the fucking Middlesbrough players were and more importantly, where they were going. It was like I'd electronically tagged them. After they'd beaten Gal and Steve to a fucking pulp I was able to follow them, with my eyes, and see which changing-room they went into.

It was the one marked 'Away' and all that remained for us to do now was fucking get in there and see to those cunts good 'n' proper, something we did with extra gusto seeing as how they'd just fucking kicked the cunting crap out of two of our own. We really fucking let them have it. They weren't just black and blue all over by the time we'd finished, they were black and blue all under as well. They were a mess of broken bones and broken spirits, about as able to kick a football as I was to not kick in some cunt who called me a cunt.

Crawling out onto the pitch, they looked a fucking

sorry sight. Or so I was told. By then, I was fucking rucking away in the stands, keeping my mind fully on that job.

I reckoned we'd more than done our bit to keep Chels in the First Division, but apparently they were so shit that season that even playing against 11 players who were on life-support machines, they only managed to win 1–0. Still, a win is a win is not a defeat, so I reckoned our 'fan' friend would be pleased. But the cunt only wasn't.

'We were two down from the first leg, so needed to win by at least two clear goals to avoid going down,' he said to me next time I saw him, which was twelve years later at a Tammy Wynette concert in Taunton.

Well, that was fucking gratitude for you and even though I was a lot older and wiser, I was still a fucking rock-hard cunt. I snuck out of the concert, rang as many of the lads as I could and told them to get down there fucking pronto. When the cunt came out of the concert I was waiting for him. And so was Gal, Steve, Gal, Steve, Gal, Steve and Sharon (as Steve was now called).

I don't think I need to tell you what happened next, but if you want to know, send a letter to the fan cunt and ask him yourself; the address is Coma Ward, Hospital For Cunts, Taunton.

chapter fucking fifteen

Boredom: it's fucking boring and no mistake. Presumably that's why it's called boredom. No one fucking likes the cunt, not even Yids. In fact, it's the fucking cunt to end all cunts, the only reason why people do anything. If boredom wasn't so fucking boring, no one would fucking do anything, would they? They'd be fucking happy enough being bored. It's what we're all fucking fighting against, in our own ways, though how some cunts find an escape from boredom by watching football or making fucking scale models of the Clifton fucking Suspension Bridge with matchsticks or having someone shit in their mouths is fucking beyond me. (Though if I was doing the shitting it might make it a bit more interesting, I suppose.) There's only one answer to boredom as far as I'm concerned: fucking kicking the shit out of some cunt. That always does it for me, conse-fucking-quently, I'm not bored very often. But when I am, Jesus, I am. It's like a fucking lead weight weighed down with more lead weights which themselves are weighed down with yet more lead weights attached to my head which itself is enclosed in a crash helmet made out of lead and filled with water. But it's only not fucking real, is it, this crash helmet, so I can't fucking just take it off, can I? It's not a fucking itch that I can fucking scratch and it fucks off, it's like an itch that I *can't* fucking scratch, even with a fucking long stick or a machete, and it just keeps on fucking itching. Itching, itching, itching, the whole fucking time.

Course, as I've said, the antidote to boredom for me is rucking. Even the thought of rucking gets rid of the boredom and, if I can imagine it vividly enough, replaces it with a fucking hard-on. Yeah, I'm not ashamed to fucking admit it, I've wanked to the thought of me rucking, come in fucking torrents, I have, imagining the lead that was making my head so fucking heavy being transferred to my toecaps and my toecaps being transferred to some cunt's head and his head fucking splitting open and fucking raspberry juice pouring out fucking everywhere and me fucking carrying on fucking kicking and kicking and kicking and more fucking rosewater splashing out and then fucking brains pouring out over my fucking boots and me kicking harder and harder and harder and harder and harder. Yeah. Fucking great. Read that and wank.

The very best cure for boredom, though, is rucking at football. I'll be honest, sometimes when I've been rucking elsewhere, maybe in the pub, at a wedding, in the steam room at a Turkish baths, sometimes I find myself becoming a little detached. Ironic, really, as parts of the cunt I'm seeing to will also become detached, but in a different way. It's not that I'm not totally fucking focused on the damage I'm inflicting; as I explained in the last chapter, as a top boy, I couldn't afford not to be, it's that I'm giving it my all, 100 fucking per cent, and I'm aware that I'm not fucking enjoying it as much as I fucking should be, aware that somewhere that cunt boredom is creeping in and sucking my fun away. It's kind of inevitable, really; when you've laid into as many cunts as I have, once in a blue fucking moon it's going to feel a bit samey, isn't it? Sometimes I almost wish the cunt I'm kicking in would surprise me and fucking give me a slap back, but I'm so fucking hard that never happens.

But at football, with the game going on, the Old Bill piling in, the noise, the smells, the smelly noise, the television cameras, the Bovril and the scarves, I'm never fucking bored rucking. Never. Ever. Never ever. Ever.

Which makes it quadruply fucking annoying, maybe even quintupletly fucking annoying, when there's a no-show from the firm you're meant to be having it out with. It's bang bang bang bang bang out of order. One, it defeats the whole fucking point of going to football, and two, it means that unless we can find some other cunts to ruck with, the icy chill of boredom is going to come lactating down upon us. And that means boredom.

That season, 1988–89, was a big no-show season. Some firms had the decency to turn up, yer Birminghams and yer Manchester Citys. Even those fucking educated Oxford cunts came and had a go because they thought they were hard enough. (They weren't.) But the likes of yer Shrews-fucking-burys and yer Wal-fucking-salls, who Chelsea were playing for some reason, did those cunts bother to come and do their civic fucking duty and try and take the Shed? No, they only fucking did fucking not, didn't they? They didn't even bring one single solitary cunt down to stand in the North Stand and get his head kicked in. Not one. To be honest, it showed them up for the thick cunts they were, cause we'd only fucking stick it to them twice as bad when we went up there, but down at the Bridge, it was a problem. A problem that needed solving with a solution that would solve it.

It first reared its pug-ugly head at half-time in the Walsall game. Usually at that time, we'd have been tearing into the cunts and fucking making them wish they hadn't bothered coming, but it very quickly became abun-fucking-dant-fucking-ly clear that it was a massive no-show. At first, we couldn't fucking believe it.

'I can't fucking believe it,' said Gal.

'Neither can I,' said Steve.

'Nor I,' said Gal.

'Me either,' said Gal.

'Or me,' said Gal.

'What about you, Steve?' I said.

'No, I can't believe it either,' he said.

So that was that. None of us could believe it. And it also soon became clear that none of the lads from the other Chelsea firms could believe it either.

'Look,' cried Donkey Dave, a quasi-neo-faux face from another firm.

We all turned to look in the direction in which he had just gesticulated wildly. There, approaching the Fulham Road and heading towards the ground, was a large, black, dense cloud of pure top-grade, 100-per-cent-proof boredom. And it was moving fast.

Quick as a flash, we put our collective hooligan heads together in a sort of mass head-butt, desperate to find some way of forcing the boredom back from where it had come – Totteridge and Whetstone, I think. Some wise guy suggested that there had to be a few Walsallian cunts somewhere in the ground and we should go round kicking the shit out of anyone who even vaguely resembled or sounded like one, but none of us knew what the cunts looked or sounded like, we didn't even know where fucking Walsall was, for fuck's sake, so that was a non-starter. A few of the other lads kicked shit out of the cunt who'd suggested that for suggesting that, but it was such a minor ruck, a scuffle, really, that it didn't divert the boredom at all.

As the second half kicked off, the cloud was almost upon us. Where there should have been an intense adrenalin high fuelled by the mullahing of some cunts, there was only the aching adrenalin low of the non-mullahing of no cunts. The Old Bill fucking loved it. They fucking loved it, the cunts. Loved seeing us suffer. Fuck, they were sick bastards. If the cloud hadn't been practically enveloping us, we might have just had it out with some of them and be done with it, but by now, hardened fucking hard nuts were looking down at the ground and idly kicking bits of gravel. Hands that should have been clenched in fist-like fists and punching some cunt's fucking head were firmly in pockets, absent-mindedly scratching scrotums. It was a sorry, sorry sight. The end they were at was so loose it was almost unattached.

I too could feel myself falling under the spell of the bastard boredom. My mind was dulling over. I had to act fast – a whole afternoon's enjoyment was at stake, for Christ's sake.

What happened next will stay in my memory and the memory of all who were there that day for the rest of this year and possibly until next spring. From deep, deep inside my vocal cavity, where my spleen meets my nemus of ocllaville, a movement started. Slowly, it made its way up. Up, up, up. Past my left lung, past my right lung. Past my aorta. Past my uncular presticle. Through my right ventricle, over my ides of membes, into my kidney chamber it went. Reaching my St Pancreas, it headed left to the patella, via my femeric muscle. As it passed over my diaphragm it began to take shape. Up, up it continued, annoyingly popping in to see both hemispheres of my brain, my hypothalamus and my visual cortex before popping back down to my left lung to get something it had forgotten.

Finally, it reached the back of my throat. Moments later, it had spewed out of my mouth as the following: 'We're the middle, we're the middle, we're the middle of the Shed.'

It took a moment for the full effect of what I'd said to take full effect, but slowly, I could see realisation dawning, and we all fucking know that realisation dawning is the neme-fucking-sis of boredom setting. Seconds later, the retort I'd been hoping and praying for boomed out.

'We're the west side, we're the west side, we're the west side of the Shed.'

It was the call to arms I'd been waiting for, the one that told me and all who were with me in the middle of the Shed that we now had an enemy, and one who had fucking bothered to show. But it only fucking got better, didn't it?

'We're the east side, we're the east side, we're the east side of the Shed.'

Two enemies now. It was more than I could have hoped for in my wildest dreams that weren't about sex.

It was incredible. Like an amoeba, we'd acted with base instinct and split into three. Three factions. Three *opposing* factions. We were the middle of the shed and the other two, well, fuck them, they weren't us, so they were cunts who deserved to have their fucking heads kicked in.

With undisguised glee, we piled into those east-side-of-the-Shed and west-side-of-the-Shed cunts. At the same time, the east-side-of-the-Shed cunts piled into the west-side-of-the-Shed cunts and vice versa. Truth be told, it was hard to fully gauge where the middle of the shed ended and the east or west side of the shed started, which meant we might well have been piling into some middle-of-the-Shed cunts as well, but, as I've made clear on many an occasion, a cunt is a cunt is a cunt, so who gives a fuck?

The whole thing went off fucking big time and fucking wiped the smile off the Old Bill's face good 'n' proper style, meaning that they had to pile in as well. Out of nowhere, I'd conjured up an almighty fucking set-to. As I charged into a group of east-side-of-the-Shed cunts, I was almost pleased that the Walsall cunts hadn't shown, though that wasn't going to get them off the hook next time we were up there.

I was carried out of the ground on the shoulders of my deliriously happy mates that day. From then on, whenever there was a no-show by some cunts, we would know what to do: separate off into arbitrary factions and kick the living crap out of each other. As they carried me in the direction of The Cum-Splattered Spittoon and Inkwell for a post-ruck drink (and hopefully ruck), I fancied I could see a large, black cloud heading off in the direction of Walsall; but, not knowing exactly where Walsall was, I wasn't 100 per cent certain.

chapter fucking sixteen

'We had joy, we had fun, we had Arsenal on the run, but the joy didn't last cause the bastards ran too fast.' I fucking made that up and any cunt who says otherwise is a cunt. 'Hit him on the head, hit him on the head, hit him on the head with a baseball bat, on the head, on the head.' That was me too. 'You're gonna get your fucking head kicked in.' Mine. 'Yiiiiiiiiddddddoooooooooooo.' Me. There were others as well that didn't quite make the grade: 'Cunts, cunts, you're all a bunch of cunts,' that was one, and 'Hello, hello, Chelsea aggravation, Chelsea aggravation, hello,' that was another. I don't know what it was about that one, but I just couldn't quite get the fucker to work and then some other cunt fucking adapted it a little and tried to pass it off as his own. Only tracked the cunt down, didn't I, and after we'd had a little 'chat' he agreed to a 60/40 royalty split, in my favour (and I agreed to a 100 per cent skull split in his favour).

Yeah, that season my chants-to-accompany-violence production really fucking skyrocketed. Well, I had a lot of time on my hands, see, on account of my being fucking banged up. That's right, you heard right, in your head that is, in the form of thoughts. Banged up. In-fucking-carcerated. Having a holiday at her majesty's pleasure, and expense.

It was fucking stupid, really. No, it was worse than that, it was really fucking really stupid. And it only had nothing to do with football, didn't it? It was like that gangster cunt in the '20s, Al Capone. He fucking wasted a ton of cunts, with violins or something like that, but at the end of the day, he only got put away for some cunting tax reason, didn't he? That's why I was always doubly careful with my tax returns, always made fucking certain all those affairs were bang in double-entry order. Cause you got to learn from the past, right, from other cunts' mistakes. Al, or Alan as I call him, was a top boy in his manor. All right, he wasn't a top boy in football, in fact, if he'd come down our way, lording it about with his 'I'm a top boy in my manor' ways, I'd have fucking sorted the cunt good 'n' proper and shown him he was well short of being a top boy in football. But he didn't. He stayed well fucking clear.

My mistake had nothing to do with tax. It was my TV fucking licence. I'd only fucking forgotten to renew it, hadn't I? Got three fucking years. Bit steep, really, but then I did fucking mullah the two licence detector cunts who turned up at my door one night, which made me feel a little better about it.

It was late. I'd been down The Aaaaarrrrgggghhhhhhhh Fuck Off And Leave Me Alone and Jumbo Jet with Gal, Steve, Steve, Steve and Steve. It had been a fucking top night as it goes. A group of tourist cunts from somewhere that wasn't England were drinking in the boozer when we arrived. Only fucking turned to look at us when we walked in, didn't they? Got what they deserved and a half, all 19 of them. Taught them a valuable lesson, we did. Next time they go to a foreign country they'll have the decency to learn about its customs first and not fucking go round insulting the locals, will they, though I doubt they ventured out of their front doors again after the kicking we gave them.

We also taught a lesson to some cunt who spilled my pint. Well, when I say he spilled my pint, he didn't, but he might as well have done. If a butterfly flapping its wings in China can bring down the fucking Berlin Wall, then him breathing over the other side of the pub can fucking spill my pint, and I, for one, wasn't going to let him continue breathing and chance that happening.

So it had been a good night and one that I was hoping to round off with an almighty wank back home. I was shacked up with some bird at the time, but luckily, she'd fucked off to a domestic violence refuge, so I had the run of the place. I cracked a beer and put a tape of a fucking massive off that went off when Millwall played Luton a couple of years back into the video. I was just unbuttoning the first button on my Levi 10101929382s when there was a knock at the door.

'Fuck me,' I thought. 'Those tourist cunts have only regrouped and come back for more. Fucking great.'

As far as I was concerned, a good night was about to get even better.

Remembering to redo my button up and replace my semi-erect cock, I charged to the door and flung it open.

'Come on then! Who wants some?' I screamed at the top of my voice, or just below it, as I didn't want to wake the neighbours.

'Mr Fist?' said a bespectacled cunt standing in the doorway next to another bespectacled cunt.

I looked behind them. No sign of the other tourist cunts. I looked to their left. No sign of the other tourist cunts. I looked to their right. No sign of the other tourist cunts. I looked above them. No sign of the other tourist cunts. I even ripped up the fucking floorboards and looked below them, but there was still no sign of the other tourist cunts.

'What the fuck have you done with those tourist cunts, you cunts?' I bellowed at the be-glasses-ed pair of cunts.

'I beg your pardon?' said the one who'd previously said 'Mr Fist?' 'We don't know about any tourists, we're from the television licensing authority and we have reason to believe that you're operating a television set without a licence.'

I looked at the cunt with my best 'You what? What the cunting fuck are you fucking well on about, mate?' face.

The other cunt read my face well.

'There's no point denying it, albeit non-verbally,' he said. 'We can detect one of those mini hand-held portable tellies from 500 yards away, even if it's been stuffed in a duvet, wrapped in masking tape and placed in an underground nuclear shelter.'

They were clearly giving me the old good TV licence man, bad TV licence man routine, but it wasn't going to work. No fucking way. Those cunts had picked the wrong guy, in the wrong house, in the wrong street, in the wrong manor, in the wrong town, on the wrong night.

'You think there's a fucking telly in here then, do you?' I said, my brain working overtime and time and a half. 'Well, why don't you fucking come in and see if you can see it?'

I purposely put extra emphasis on the word 'see' cause I knew what was going to happen, didn't I? I like to think that when the four-eyed tossers looked back on the incident, perhaps at some point during the years of fucking therapy they will have needed to get over it, maybe they realised I did that and had a bit of a chuckle about it.

Like the stupid bastards they were, they both walked into the gaff and headed for the lounge. The tape I'd put on had rewound now and the sound of football violence, a sort of group version of the unmistakeable 'It's about to go off' sound, was blaring out of the telly.

'There, Mr Fist,' said one of the cunts, I forget which one. 'If I'm not very much mistaken, that is a television set.'

He then turned to look at his colleague and the faintest of faint smirks tremoloed across his face. If previously there had been the slightest possibility of any mercy being shown on my behalf, which there wasn't, he had just been a party to it vanishing altogether.

'Well,' I said, raising myself up to my full 5 ft 7 in. and puffing out my chest like one of those blower fish inhaling during a hurricane, 'I think you *are* very much mistaken. Why don't you have another look?'

'Mr Fist, I really don't think there's any need—' he started saying. But somewhere in that sentence, probably just after he'd said 'need', otherwise I wouldn't have written it, the bottle of beer I'd been drinking found its way into his face. Well, when I say bottle, it was more like half of the bottle, and as luck would have it, it was the broken half that found his face first.

With the half-bottle embedded between his eyes such that the neck protruded outwards, like an extra nose dripping snot on to my carpet – in fact, it was beer not snot that was ruining my carpet, something I tried to claim for when I later sued the authorities – I politely asked the cunt again.

'Now then, you cunt, can you see a telly in here?'

Funnily enough, this time he couldn't. (I'm not so sure he'll chuckle about that 'see' when he relives it in therapy.) And neither could his cunt of a mate. Maintaining my politeness, I thanked them for coming and showed them the door.

Twenty minutes later, I only found myself in the back of a Black Maria on the way to the nick, didn't I? Some cunt had fucking grassed me up. To this day, I don't know who it was, but if I ever find out, they are fucking dead. The nearest I came to finding out was a couple of years back when Gal told me he reckoned he knew, but that made him a grass so I fucking mullahed him. Yeah: never, ever grass. Even if you're grassing up a grass, or grassing up the grass who grassed up a grass, or grassing up the grass who grassed up the grass who grassed up a grass, fucking don't do it.

'Guilty.' No cunt wants to hear that word, do they? It's right up there with 'You've got cancer', 'What do you mean you can't get a hard-on?' and 'Excuse me, have you got the time?' But hear it I did. Followed by 'three years'. (Not directly followed by 'three years', but I'm not fucking writing everything down, you fill in the fucking blanks.)

Going to nick didn't bother me. In fact, I was quite looking forward to it: three meals a day, a roof over my head and loads of fucking cunts to ruck with. What did bother me was not going to football – that bothered me.

'Who's the Daddy?' I said to the guvnor on my first day inside. 'Who's number one, who's una paloma blanca, who's Darth Vader?'

He was clearly impressed by my grasp of prison lingo and, fixing me with a hot, soft stare, said, 'It's Gory Gal the Greenwich Greaser.'

'That ponce,' I said. 'Well, tell him from me, his days are numbered, there's a new kid on the block.'

'Why don't you tell him yourself?' said the guvnor.

'Hello, Steve,' said a voice behind me. 'Long time no see.'

I swung round, fully expecting to see the ugly mug of Gory Gal the Greenwich Greaser. But it was only Gal, wasn't it? Gal who'd got banged up when it went off with the Taff Old Bill in Swansea. He'd been transferred down to this nick and was now fagging for the guvnor. I should have known it was too much of a coincidence for the guvnor to say 'Why don't you tell him yourself?' and for Gory Gal the Greenwich Greaser to actually be there himself and then say 'Hello, Steve' at that exact moment. That sort of thing only happens in films.

'Fuck off Gal, you cunt,' I said. 'Me and the guvnor got some business to sort out.'

Gal scurried out in the way only cunts can.

Ten minutes later, I was standing in Gory Gal the Greenwich Greaser's cell, on Gory Gal the Greenwich Greaser's head.

'OK, OK, yes,' he screamed from beneath my prison-regulation 7-holed marmalade-toe-capped DMs.

Eleven minutes later, I was standing in *my* cell, on Gory Gal the Greenwich Greaser's head. It felt good to be the top boy once again; pride coursed through my veins like a hare on roller skates on heroin with a rocket up its arse. I leant down to Gory Gal the Greenwich Greaser's head.

'Your face is fucking ruining my DMs,' I said. 'That's going to cost you a sherbet dib-dab.'

It was the final humiliation for the cunt. Inside, sherbet dib-dabs, or anal shooty bootys as they were sometimes called, were the most sought after items. They were similar to street sherbet dib-dabs, but rather than pour the sherbet into your mouth, in the nick you got some cunt to blow it up your arse whilst simultaneously tickling your bollocks with the liquorice. Gory Gal the Greenwich Greaser knew that cunt was going to be him.

With that little problem sorted, I dived headlong into the bigger problem of football.

It didn't take long to suss out that the cons in the nick had already divided themselves into football gangs. There was a bunch of Arsenal cons, Tottenham cons, Leeds cons, West Ham cons, Brechin City cons and Manchester United cons. They all had their own areas of the nick and the exercise yard, as well as small shares in the prison delicatessen, an enterprise that had been set up to better prepare prisoners who were to be released into North London for life on the outside.

As long as the gangs kept themselves to themselves, all was dory and all was hunky. But if a young sapling – prison slang for cunt – strayed into another's territory, all fucking, cunting hell broke loose, and before you knew where you were, everyone was up on the roof and smearing shit everywhere in a massive cunting dirty protest and banging their plates and cutlery on the tables at mealtimes and holding screws to ransom. It was a delicate balance all right, but that suited me fine. Society had seen fit to strip me of my regular weekly dose of football violence on the outside, so in order not to become one of those cunts who become institutionalised and can't function when they're released and find themselves trapped in a cycle of going to prison, getting released from prison, going to prison, getting released from prison, going to prison, getting released from prison, going to prison, getting released from prison and then going to prison again, it was my duty to ensure a massive football-related fucking ruck took place every fucking week. I mean, otherwise I'd just come out and be like a cunt out of water and end up becoming a burden to society.

The first thing I needed to do was sort out a Chelsea firm. Apart from a couple of screws, there weren't any Chels in the nick, so the next time Steve, Steve and Gal came to see me, I had a word.

'Right, lads, listen up, some lag in this shithole has only gone and blabbed about a nice little number down in Guildford.'

The lads looked at me blankly.

'Sorry, Steve, you what, mate?' said Steve.

I'd only forgotten that they didn't speak prison lingo, hadn't I?

'Right, lads,' I said, for a second time, 'some cunt in this nick has only gone and fucking told me about a building society in Guildford that is fucking ripe for a going over. Reckons we can stroll in and help ourselves to 25 large no problem.'

Now the lads understood me and I could tell by the way they all hugged each other and started limbo dancing that they were excited by the idea, or at least what they thought was the idea.

'I want you to get all the fucking lads in on it, right, Gal?' I said to Gal.

'Right,' Gal said back to me.

I gave them all the details, the wheres, the whens, the whos, the hows, the dos, the don'ts, the whys and the perhapses and off they went. Then I called one of the screws over.

'Oi, screw cunt, here a minute.'

'Yeah, what is it?' he said. He was obviously new to the job. I flashed him my number-one badge.

'Sorry,' he said. 'How can I be of assistance?'

'That's better,' I barked. 'Now listen. I just got wind of a job going down tomorrow night in Guildford. The Halifax on the High Street. A call from you to the right people, the sort of people who can arrange a little welcoming party for the slags involved, and I reckon a promotion might be on the cards.'

Oh, I could be a smooth-talking fucker when I wanted to be and no mistake. After a little confusion about whether it was a Guildford Building Society in Halifax or a Halifax Building Society in Guildford, the screw cunt had it sorted in his screw cunt head and went off to make that call. By the end of that week, all the lads were with me in the nick – apart from Gal, the stupid cunt had gone to Halifax – and there was a new Chelsea gang, ready for action.

Truth be told, most of the boys were happy to be inside. On the outside, without me at the helm, a lot of them had gone to pieces, some of them hadn't even had a ruck in three days, for fuck's sake. Others had wandered the streets forlorn and lost, forgetting to eat, drink, shit and breathe, mumbling incoherently. I was their lifeblood, the placenta at the end of their umbilical cord but not one they had any chance of ever frying with onions and eating.

'Fucking cheers, lads,' I said, raising my pint aloft.

'Cheers,' said Gal.

'Cheers,' said Gal.

'Cheers,' said Gal.

'Cheers,' said Steve.

'Cheers,' said Gal.

'Cheers,' said Gal.

We were having a drink down the prison boozer, The

Gay Gay Gay Gay Gay Gay Gay and Hydrogen Bomb. Course, it wasn't a real boozer, it was Steve the Stockwell Strangler's cell, but he'd done it up so that it had a certaine olde worlde charme and made some pop out of rat's intestines, dandruff and the deputy guvnor's wife's quim juice. It wasn't bad, actually, better than most of those fucking bottled foreign lagers. The screws turned a blind eye to it, even tossing us the odd new boy from time to time to beat the shit out of and anally rape. I gave the lads their instructions.

'First thing tomorrow, Gal, you sort out our area of the exercise yard. Steve, you organise a place on the wing that we can call our own and Gal, you're in charge of the deli. Any part is fine as long as there's no olive fucking tapenade in it, I hate the cunting stuff. Got it?'

The lads all nodded, though for some reason not in unison but one after the other.

'Now then,' I continued, the lads hanging both on and off my every word, 'that'll cover the majority of rucks. If any cunt so much as dreams about any of our territory, we fucking sort them. But if we're to stand any chance of integrating back into society when we get out, any chance' – I said it again in case the cunts were in some doubt as to the seriousness of the matter – 'any chance at all' – I said it a third time and added 'at all' to really ram home my point – 'we've got to sort the football.'

'So, what're we going to do then, Steve?' said Steve.

He was trying to sound calm, nonchalant, as if the

question was more a gentle enquiry than something upon which the stability of the entire rest of his life depended. But I knew him better than that. I knew them all better than that, apart from Gal. And Gal.

'Well,' I said, leaning back and filling my pipe with a particularly rich shag I'd 'acquired' off of some ponce on E By Gum Wing, 'what we do is this.'

The plan I'd come up with was ingenious in its simplicity, yet simple in its ingeniousness. Back then, there wasn't that much football on telly because the radio owned most of the rights to it. Course, unknown to us doing bird, that was all about to change. But the only information we got from the outside consisted of tiny scraps of The Sun smuggled in up the arse of a new con or a visitor – it was like reading shit covered in shit – so we weren't to know.

The radio covered all the fucking games of a Saturday and that meant all we had to do was listen to it to find out what the fuck was going on. Literally. Those radio-commentating cunts' words were going to provide us with the exact instructions we needed.

Getting a radio wasn't a problem. I was number one, the Daddy, Oppo Del Oppo, Top Cat. If I needed something doing, it got done, otherwise some cunt got a right fucking going over and no mistake. As it turned out, there were a couple of geezers on the wing who wore glasses, which meant they were brainy and would be able to make a radio, which they did. They fashioned it out of a ladle that Gal stole from the kitchen and a pair of secateurs that he didn't. The antenna was placed in some nonce's arse, which afforded us a fair reception, though his bollocks got in the way and meant we couldn't always get Radio 4.

The following Saturday in the exercise yard, everything was in place. I had two teams of cons on a makeshift football pitch waiting on every fucking word that was about to come out of that radio.

It cackled into life like an old crone of a witch with a particularly big frog in her throat, sending little jolts of electricity through the nonce, something I reckon the fucking cunt quite liked.

'Thank you, John, and welcome to Stamford Bridge for today's game between Chelsea and Manchester City. Chelsea have won the toss and will be kicking off playing from left to right as we look.'

The 11 cons representing Chelsea looked over to me. From where I was, if they kicked off, they'd be playing from right to left; either they had to change position with the cons representing Manchester City, or else I had to change my perspective so that they would be playing from left to right as I looked.

It was no contest. Those cunts moved and I stayed right where I fucking was.

'Chelsea sticking with their familiar 4-4-2 formation that has served them so well this season, whilst City look like they'll be playing 5-3-2. Should be an interesting game, Jimmy?'

I wasn't interested in what any cunt called Jimmy said.

Whilst he waffled on about some fucking shit, the two teams of cons sorted out their formations. Then we were off.

'Speedie kicks off for Chelsea and lays the ball back to Nevin who lofts it forward.'

Immediately the teams of cons did as the commentator cunt said.

'Quinn wins it in the air and it falls to Sheron who lays it wide to Brightwell.'

It only worked a fucking treat, didn't it? Cause radio's predominantly an aural medium, the fucking commentary had to explain what the fuck was going on on the pitch, didn't it? OK, so some of the players who didn't get mentioned felt about as useful as a dildo in a bread-basket, but the important action was being fucking described for us and that was fucking good enough for me. Ten minutes into the game, we made our move.

Some cunts from Jazzy B Wing who had agreed to be a firm from Man City had gathered behind the goal City were defending. Like panthers on those hoverboards out of *Back to the Future*, we stealthily made our way round to where they were standing and, using a combination of brute force and osmosis, infiltrated their number.

'Beautiful control by White,' said the radio, or, more precisely, said the commentator cunt on the radio. 'He's found Heath in space on the right, still Heath, still Heath, must be . . . ohhhh, just wide.'

It was the moment I'd been waiting for. As the commentator cunt had ohhhed so had the City firm.

They'd only fucking revealed themselves. Now it was time to reveal ourselves, though not in the way the nonce would have wanted us to.

'Chhhheeelllllsseeeeaaaa!' I roared.

And with that, all fucking hell broke loose. We fucking kicked shit out of those cunts and chased them down a structurally identical Fulham Road some bent town planners in the nick had built, after getting planning permission. It was fucking magic seeing the boys in action again and I was particularly pleased with the two Chelsea screws, who delivered a savage beating to the con playing one of City's top boys.

The following week, Chelsea were away to Liverpool and once again, as the radio commentary kicked off, so did we. It was a fucking revelation, so fucking good that I considered murdering some other con so that I could get my sentence extended and enjoy the delights of kicking the cunting shit out of some cunt by radio for longer. In the end, I didn't because I realised that all the other lads would also have to murder someone so that they could stay inside and that if they did that, we'd be short of cons to play the actual game. It was one of those in-fucking-tractable problems, like what happens when a fucking immovable object meets an unstoppable fucking force – 'Who gives a fuck?' is the answer – so I left it.

With the football problem sorted, I could enjoy my three years reha-fucking-bilitation. Course we had the odd problem or two, like when the nonce shat himself during a

Cup tie at Wigan or when the commentator cunts made a mistake in their commentary and we'd already acted it out, but on the whole it ran like clock-fucking-work.

At the end of my sentence, I was good and ready to retake my rightful place in society, secure in the knowledge that I would slot back in like a Tetris brick floating gently into a space. Seamless, it was going to be. No fucking halfway fucking house for me. No fucking looking like some fashion throwback and going into a newsagent and asking for a sweet that doesn't exist any more and trying to find the labour exchange. Fuck that.

'See you at the match on Saturday,' said one of the Chelsea screws as he handed me back the possessions I'd handed in three years ago – half a crown and a packet of Spangles. 'It'll be good to fucking steam in for real.'

'Fucking right,' I said. 'Twelve in The Bing Bong Bum Bum and Shut It, You Slag.'

'I'll be there, Steve,' he said.

Then I was out. I took a deep sniff of the air, or inhaled, if you like. It smelt good – fetid, but good. It was a reminder that they might be able to take away my freedom, but they can't take away the air. I strolled down the street feeling 5 ft 7 in. tall. Moments later, I'd had a ruck with two cunts who looked like they were possibly about to consider looking at me and felt even better.

'Yeah,' I thought to myself, 'thanks, Your Majesty, it certainly has been a pleasure.'

chapter fucking seventeen

'So, who is it this Saturday?' I said to Gal.

I was down The Does Exactly What It Says It Does On The Tin and Disputed Region Of Nagorno-Karabakh with the lads, having our first pints as free men in three years. Prison was already a distant memory, albeit one that we could remember incredibly well, as we'd only been out for five minutes.

Looking around, it seemed as if nothing much had changed. October 1994 didn't seem all that different to October 1991. OK, so I didn't know all the fucking songs on the jukebox, and I wasn't that fucking familiar with the computer program the landlord had installed to operate the lighting rig in the gaff, and some of the newer synthetic fibres used in the hosiery being worn by the birds had escaped my fucking attention, but funda-fucking-mentally, all was as it should be. But by fucking cunting Jesusing cunting bollocking fucking shitting cunty fucking Christ, was I wrong.

Gal ran his fingers along the Braille version of the Chelsea fixture list. He wasn't blind, he'd just never learned to read any other way.

'It's only fucking West Ham,' he said as his stubby, cigarette-stained fingers excitedly felt the tiny little metallic cigarette-stained nodules protruding up from the paper.

West Ham. Now that was what I fucking called freedom, having it out with those cunts. Immediately, we all started gabbing wildly about the damage we were going to inflict on those fuckers and telling tales of past inflictions of damage on the very same cunts. It was in the midst of Steve telling us about the time he'd single-handedly sorted out 14 of the cunts after coming across them while he was queuing overnight for the Harrods sale that Gal let rip with his bombshell.

'Fuck me,' he said.

We stopped talking instantly and froze as if at the point in a game of musical statues where the music has just been turned off. Everyone then said, 'What?'

'We're not playing on Saturday,' he said.

Again, like *Groundhog Day*, only more like groundhog second, everyone said, 'What?'

'The fucking game's only on Sunday,' Gal said, his

disbelief causing him to splutter and emit large droplets of spittle.

A silence fell on the room as if it had fallen out of the top a very tall tree, possibly one of those giant redwoods.

'You fucking what?' I bellowed eventually, shattering the silence into a million smaller pieces of silence.

'Straight up, Steve,' said Gal, producing yet more spittle. 'Feel it for yourself.'

He passed me the Braille fixture list. Course, I couldn't read the cunt, but I didn't want to look like a cunt in front of all those other cunts, so I had a feel. And anyway, I reckoned, if the blind could fucking read it, how hard could it be?

'Fuck me,' I said as my freshly manicured fingers caressed the protrusions. 'The cunt's only fucking right, isn't he?'

Truth be told, I had no fucking idea whether he was right, wrong or simply plain mistaken, I just went with my gut instinct.

'It must be a mistake,' said Steve.

Well, that was fucking it, wasn't it? I pulled a screwdriver out of my jacket and fucking laid into Steve. The cunt had only tried to show me up, in front of my mates an' all.

'No,' he screamed as punches and the shaft of a Phillips screwdriver hailed down on him, '*you* haven't made a mistake, the cunts who wrote that fucking fixture list must have made a mistake, that's what I meant.'

That stopped me in my tracks. But then I carried on pummelling the cunt until all that was left of him was a pool of foul-smelling urine. Like that cunt on Mastermind, I always finish what I start.

Fact was, he'd had a point. We got another round in and decided there and then to find out who wrote the Braille fixture list and sort them out good 'n' proper even if they were blind, in which case we'd also sort their fucking guide dog an' all.

The following Saturday, as it was West Ham, we'd treated ourselves to a drink up West, in some classy boozer that put on strip shows, The Get Your Tits Out For The Lads and Derek Nimmo, I think it was called. The birds were fucking dog-rough, but most of them had tits so it was worth it.

Tanked up, we piled out of the gaff and headed down the Tube. There was no sign of any West Ham, or any other Chels for that matter, but that didn't bother us, we were blinded by cocksureness and the headiness of freedom.

At Fulham Broadway, we stormed out of the station. It felt great to be back, leading my troops into battle.

'Cheeeeelllllllsssassseeeeeeeaaaaaaaa!' I roared like a returning king of the jungle.

I looked around, expecting others from within a swaying, pulsating mob of humanity on their way to Chels to pick up on my roar and return it, and for any West Ham in the vicinity to fucking run like the bottling slags they are. But all I got was a big, fat, overweight, podgy, chubby nothing. I felt the adrenalin drain from my body and then return, but in a different form: panic.

Then it hit me. The place was humming. Humming like a ghost town. It was fucking dead. A lifeless, sorry wind blew through the place. If it had been the Wild West 150 years earlier, a shutter would have been banging against a wall and a gunfighter would have appeared in front of us. But it wasn't. Where there should have been the electrifying buzz of the pre-football crowd were just two middle-aged ladies doing a bit of shopping and a street sweeper, whose age I could not be certain of. Not exactly West Ham's top firm, though probably just as hard.

In a flash, ironically a blinding one, I realised the cunt who'd written the Braille fixture list had not made a fucking mistake. (And neither had I, or Gal for that matter.) There was only no fucking game on.

For a moment, we all stood there, wondering and wandering. In hindsight, and foresight, I should have fucking seen it as the warning sign it was. But sometimes when the fucking bleeding obvious is screaming right in your face, like the poltergeist in that scene from *Poltergeist*, you just don't see it. If the bleeding obvious had fucking screamed in Braille, maybe we would have seen it, but it didn't. I pointed to the middle-aged ladies and the street sweeper of indeterminate age.

'Fucking kill the cunts,' I ordered.

If I'm totally fucking honest, I felt a tinge of regret

about that. I mean, for all I knew they could have been Chels, but the lads were primed, they were ready, they wanted blood. If I hadn't sorted a ruck for them that would have made me look like a cunt for one, and for two, left them with a fucking dangerous build-up of unspent energy, and that could be deadly. Years ago, a geezer from Millwall told me about a firm who'd got themselves both tanked and tooled up to the fucking max in preparation for a massive off with some Birmingham cunts, only to take a wrong turning somewhere and end up in an empty fucking field. It was an agricultural disaster, the entire fucking wheat output of the Midlands, plus a sizeable chunk of its dairy produce, was destroyed in one fell fucking swoop as they vented their unvented ruck energy on the region's cattle.

As the street sweeper – who, by the way he put up quite a decent struggle I now reckoned to be in his early 30s – went down beneath a volley of steel-toecapped boots, I called Steve over.

'Steve, come here,' I said.

Delivering a parting blow to the cunt's scrotum, Steve trotted over.

'Yeah?' he said.

'If this gets out, if the other firms find out that on our first fucking Saturday out of nick we've been made to look like mugs by some Braille-writing slag, you know what that'll mean?'

'No,' he said, because he didn't.

'We'll be the fucking laughing stock of London, mate. Or England. Or Europe. Or even the world. Or the entire fucking universe, or galaxy, whichever cunt is bigger. So I want you to get it in writing from those middle-aged lady cunts and that street sweeper cunt that they will never, ever, never fucking mention what happened here today to any fucker ever. And fucking make sure it's legally fucking binding, all right?'

'Right,' said Steve. He'd once seen an episode of *Judge Judy* so he knew what I was on about.

'And one other thing,' I said.

'What?' he said.

'You and the others keep shtum about it an' all.'

'Keep shtum about what?' he said, something that coming from anyone else I would have taken as a clever way of telling me that he'd understood what I was on about, but coming from that thick cunt I took to mean he didn't have a fucking clue what I was fucking talking about.

After explaining it again, I was satisfied he'd got it clear in his mind and head. Now I had to get clear in my mind and head exactly what the fuck was going on. There was only one thing to do; though, as it turned out, I was going to have to do that one thing a number of times before I got any answers.

'Hello,' said a voice down the other end of a phone line, probably on a phone.

'All right?' I said. 'This is Steve Fist. Is that Amblesledge the Rectorian?'

Click, derrrrrrrrrrrrrrrrrrrrrrrrrrrrrrrrrrrrr. The other person has cleared, the other person has cleared, the other person had cleared.

The phone line went dead and then a prerecorded voice told me they'd cleared. It was the same when I rang the other top Chelsea boys, Nodder, Cretin, By-Tor the Snow Dog and the Priests of the Temple of Syrinx. (Stan the Man had committed suicide some years earlier.) There was only one top boy left to call. With no small, little, minute, minuscule amount of trepidation, I dialled the number I had for Dr Felchwarden Ph.D., MD, CUNT. I'd never liked that cunt and hated him being my last fucking chance to find out in my head and mind exactly what the fuck was going on, but like it or not like it, he *was* my last chance to find out in my head and mind exactly what the fuck was going on.

'Hello,' said a voice. Even though he'd preferred to send food parcels and copies of *The Topper* comic instead of actually coming to visit me in prison, I recognised the cunt's voice instantly. Yeah, unless someone was doing a particularly good impression, it was definitely him, Dr Felchwarden Ph.D., MD, CUNT. I had to handle the situation with a certain delicacy. If he hung up on me, I would have walked myself right into a dead-end cul de sac.

'This is Steve Fist, you cunt, and if you fucking hang up on me, I will hunt you down and eat your fucking eyelids for my supper.'

I waited. Had I struck the right balance between fearsome threatening aggression and outright homicidal insanity? There was no click. No derrrrrrrrrrrrrrrrrrrrrrrr. No the other person has cleared. It seemed I'd got it just right.

'What do you want?' he said eventually, an audible sigh audibly audible.

'What I want is this. I want to know what the fuck is going on.'

There was another sigh, just as audible. Then another. Then another and another and another. In all, he sighed for about thirty-five minutes, three minutes short of the world record held by Kao Kwim Kwunt of North Korea. Finally, he spoke.

'It's all changed. Tomorrow. You'll see.'

Then he was gone. From the end of the phone line, I don't know if he left his house.

It was a crumb. A crumb of something. The words roller-coastered around in my mind. 'It's'. 'All'. 'Changed'. 'Tomorrow'. 'You'll'. 'See'. Whichever way I looked at them, there was only one possible meaning: I would see tomorrow that everything had changed.

That night, I went to sleep, but couldn't sleep. Sleep bottled it from me, fucking ran away from me faster than the speed of light in a very fast car. Tomorrow also seemed to be fucking legging it away from me, too. I wanted the cunt to come fucking quickly so that this whole fucking mess could be sorted, but it just lay there, out of reach, refusing to come nearer. As far as I was concerned, there was still only one explanation for what had happened: the fucking cunt who wrote the Braille fixture list *had* made a mistake, but everyone had gone along with it, the players, the refs, the fans, the Football Association. It had become a mistake that couldn't be recti-fucking-fied, so that the game *had* now to be played on the Sunday. It was a one-off, one of those things that just fucking happened. But as I said before, by fucking cunting Jesusing cunting bollocking fucking shitting cunty fucking Christ, was I wrong.

Eventually, I fell into a deep, deep sleep. Fuck me, was it deep. It was like someone who couldn't sleep being thrown into the very deep end of sleep and having to sleep or swim. And in the midst of it, at a depth so deep that if I had awoken too quickly I would have got the bends, he appeared. Nutter. That fucking cunt of a father of mine.

'Oi, cunt, you fucking looking at me? Do you fucking want some? Think you're fucking hard, do you? Come on, then,' he said.

'Nutter?' I said, still groggy from sleep even though I was dreaming.

Next thing I knew, the cunt had only fucking hit me, hadn't he? Killed me dead.

'Get up, you slag,' he shouted at me.

My dream self got up.

'That's for being a cunt,' he said.

He hadn't fucking changed. Even as an archetypal figment of my imagi-fucking-nation, he was still Nutter.

'Give us a fag, you cunt,' he commanded.

I reached into my pocket and felt a packet of Benson & Hedges. I pulled out a tab and handed it to him, only when he took it, it only wasn't a fucking tab any more, was it? Now it was the Sacré Coeur in Paris. He lit it and inhaled deeply anyway. Then he started coughing. And coughing and coughing and coughing. In dream time, he coughed for seven months, three weeks, two days, five hours, fourteen minutes and eight seconds, a fortnight in real, non-sleeping time. Finally, he produced the greenest fucking flob I've ever fucking seen and spat it out. Fucking emerald it was. It flew through the air, but just before it hit me full on in the face, it changed into Dan Petrescu and fucked off.

Suddenly, I awoke drenched in olive oil and sat bolt upright in bed.

'Stupid cunt,' I said, and fell straight back to sleep.

I awoke some time later. Instantly, the dream image of Nutter flashed back into my mind.

'Stupid cunt,' I said again, and stepped into the shower.

It was now the tomorrow that Dr Felchwarden Ph.D., MD, CUNT had been talking about, but so far, not a fucking thing had changed. Perhaps Felchwarden and the others had been wrong. Perhaps, as is often the case with cunts, *they* had changed, and their new per-fucking-spective made them think that everything else had changed when in fact it hadn't.

With that comforting thought rip-roaring around my mind like an extreme-sport thought, I set off to meet the lads.

'All right, Steve?' said Gal as I hightailed it into The Dick and Dom on Dudden Hill Lane.

'Yeah, can't fucking complain,' I said. 'Everyone here?'

'Yeah,' he said, 'they're just sorting out some cunts who were being cunts in the saloon bar.'

'Well, what the fuck are you doing in here then, you fucking bottling slag heap?'

And with that, I laid into the cunt who, to give him his dues, put up a fair fight. He even managed to bite half my ear off. But only after I'd bitten his hair off, so it was something of a token effort.

Fresh from sorting out the cunts in the saloon bar, the lads returned. Now they were primed and ready for the big off with those West Ham cunts. You see that's the difference between humans and animals, that's what separates us and makes us the rulers of this fucking planet. Yer fucking lion has a ruck with an antelope or a wilde-fucking-beest and then doesn't have another ruck for three or four fucking days. They just don't understand the concept of building up to the big off, to having it out with the whole fucking herd of antelope or wilde-fucking-beest. Granted, the lion fucking eats the antelope or wilde-fucking-beest, but I reckon even if the lads had eaten those cunts in the saloon bar, they still would have wanted to go on and fucking have it out with West Ham.

Four pints and three toffee liqueur chasers later, we headed down the Tube. So far, still nothing had changed, further cementing my belief that nothing had changed and that all that had changed was those other cunts' outlooks.

Down the Tube, I was yet further reassured by the reassuring familiarity of everything. The platform and subsequent train that arrived were packed with geezers going to football. The buzz that had been so conspicuous by its not being there yesterday was most definitely there, buzzing around the train. I felt it infecting my being until every synapse in my body was crackling like bits of pork.

Arriving at Fulham Broadway, we alighted in the traditional manner, i.e. we piled out, to see that familiar throbbing mass of geezanity bobbing and weaving its way to the ground. It was a sight that would have brought tears to a less hard geezer's eyes. As my heart pounded with the certainty that all was right with my world, I inhaled deeply and, just as I had done the previous day, let out a roar.

'Cheeeeeeeeellllllllllssssssssssseeeeeeeeeeaaaaaaaaaa!'

No sooner had the last syllable of the last syllable exited my mouth, than my entire universe crumbled and I was sucked into a black hole. The earth beneath my feet gave way, the whole essence of my being shattered. Two plus two no longer equalled four. All roads did not lead to Rome. An Englishman's home was no longer his fucking castle.

The second I stopped roaring, two coppers, or, as they were now called, community fucking liaison officers, appeared.

'Sorry, sir,' said the first one, 'would you mind keeping your voice down please, there's a 40-decibel sound limit in the area on match days. Thanks for your cooperation in the matter.'

Then they both smiled at me and fucked off. No knee to the groin, no truncheon up the arse, no nothing.

Gobsmacked because I hadn't been, I turned to the lads. They were all standing in a tight-knit group staring in wide-eyed disbelief. I felt a certain warmth that they were as non-fucking-plussed by what had just happened as I was; but then I followed their gaze and realised that their wide-eyed-disbeliefness had fuck all to do with what they had just beheld happen to me, but with the scene unfolding in front them. What I saw instantly widened my eyes and made my sense became one of disbelief, too. There, right in front of us, walking side by fucking side, was a geezer in a Chelsea shirt *and* a geezer in a West Ham shirt. And they were even fucking chatting to each other. And laughing. Yes, fucking laughing. It just made no sense at all. It didn't fucking compute. By rights, they should have been fucking going at it hammer, tong, fish slice, spatula, spanner and combine harvester. They should have been desperately trying to inflict massive amounts of pain on each other. They should have been rucking.

As my eyes widened still further in yet more disbelief, only this time horizontally so I began to resemble a fucking nip, I looked around. What I wanted was proof that it was just a one-off, that they were a couple of mentals on a day trip from the fucking loony bin. But as I surveyed the greater scene, the reality dawned on me like a fucking great sun rising over the horizon that was my fucking mind. Everywhere I looked, Chels and West Ham were mingling together, walking alongside one another, happy as cunting Larry, oblivious to the great wrong they were doing. There was only one thing for it.

'Fuck me, I need a fucking drink,' I said.

Instantly, the two community liaison officers reappeared.

'I'm sorry, sir,' said the other one, 'can I just remind you that swearing is not permitted on match days. Thank you for your cooperation in the matter.'

Now I needed a fucking drink more than ever. As Felchwarden's words began to float in front of my eyes, I looked round for a welcoming boozer, an oasis of sanity in a desert of sand.

'There,' whispered Gal, not wanting to incur the wrath of the community liaison officers.

The place he pointed to was called The Guardian Reader and Chattering Classes. From the outside, it certainly resembled a boozer and, moving as an even more tight-knit group, we made our way towards it.

'Forty-seven pints,' I said to the geezer behind the bar,

desperate for the relief, numbness, escape and, at the same time, vapid familiarity that vast amounts of alcohol rapidly consumed would afford me.

'I'm terribly sorry, sir,' he said, 'we don't sell beer on match days. Perhaps I can get you a decaffeinated cappuccino. Or maybe a green tea, it's very good for you, full of antioxidants.'

That one sent me fucking reeling for fucking real. I felt like a fucking monster mule had just delivered a fucking massive kick to my nads, which, incidentally, are massive. My head started to spin like in that scene from *The Exorcist*. On the plus side, it allowed me to take a good look round the boozer; but what I saw sickened me to my stomach and beyond. A boozer is sacred territory. Summoning all the reasonableness I could fucking muster, I could just about counte-fucking-nance Chels and West Ham geezers walking together on the way to the fucking ground; maybe they just hadn't noticed each other, maybe they were lulling each other into a false sense of security and when the time was right they would fucking belt the living fuck out of each other. But if there's one fucking place that is clearly fucking demar-fucking-cated, it's the fucking boozer; a Chels boozer is a Chels boozer. Fucking end of. No fucking ifs. No buts. No fucking nothing.

But as my head spun, it became clear that even this golden fucking rule, this linch-fucking-pin of the whole fucking show, this fucking top boy philosophical fucking tenet, even that cunt had been ripped apart and given a right fucking kicking. There, there in what should have been a Chelsea boozer, right there before my rapidly revolving head, were fucking West Ham, fucking drinking. And it wasn't because they'd fucking taken the pub, steamed in and had it out with the Chels in there – the only acceptable reason they could have been in there in my rapidly crumbling world – because right fucking next to them were Chels, also fucking drinking. It was like a scene out of some fucking weird science fiction film. In fact, for a moment I thought it fucking really was a film and any moment now some cunt would shout 'cut' and we'd realise it was all part of the vivid fucking imagination of some screenwriter cunt. But no cunt shouted 'cut' and that fucking monster mule just kept delivering more and more kicks to my fucking monster nads.

The effect all this had on the lads was cata-fucking-strophic; they were approaching delirium and catatonia, and dropping like fucking flies. The tight-knit group was dropping fucking stitches left, right and centre. With the more mentally robust lads hanging on to my coat tails, I managed to stagger across the road to The Duck and Post-Modern Irony. It was the same story in there. And in The Late Show and Butternut Squash. And The Taramasalata, Halloumi Salad and Radio 4.

All down Fulham Road, in every fucking boozer, it was the same fucking story.

'I can't go on,' croaked Gal as he collapsed in the gutter.

Then Gal went. Then Steve. Then Gal, Gal, Gal, Steve, Steve, Steve, Steve and Gal. Then I was alone.

With my mind racing out of control, I did the only thing I knew how to: I fought. Fucking had it out with my mind, kicked shit out of the cunt, beat it to a pulp until the bottling bastard legged it and I was back, sure and in control. Now I knew why Nutter had come to me in the night. He had always been a one-man firm, a sole trader in the hooligan market; it was time for me to step into his shoes.

A calm, both inner and outer, descended upon me. I was now a firm. No Gal. No Steve. No Steve. No Steve. No Gal. No fucking no one but fucking me. If I was to be the last of the mohooligans, then so be it, so be fucking it.

Sticking my chest, head and left thigh out, I walked erectly to the ground. In my head, which had stopped spinning and was now gently lolling from side to side, I began to make a plan. With Chels and West Ham mingling like cunting lovers, it would be no fucking problem to infiltrate the West Ham. I'd get in there amongst them and when they least fucking expected it, I would fucking charge the cunts and run them, run them back to their fucking east London slag heaps and fucking beyond. And any Chels who were fucking with them were fucking traitors and cunts as far as I was concerned and would fucking get what was coming to them as fucking well.

Suddenly, I felt alive again. I knew there would be more unexpected Felchwarden-type changes to come, changes that would try and knock me off my perch and keep me from my task, my crusade, but I made a mental note to myself to brace myself for them and not let them deflect me from my true goal. And to be doubly certain, I also made a physical note to the same effect. As I went to get my ticket at the turnstile, the first of those changes had a pop at me.

'That'll be £3,000, please, sir,' said the turnstile operative operator.

'Free fousan' pans?' I began to exclaim, my fingers instinctively grouping together in that oh-so-familiar fist shape, ready to fucking let the cunt have one for being such a cunt.

'That's correct, sir,' he said.

Quickly, I reread my mental note to myself and then double-checked by rereading the physical note. It did the trick. My fingers disinstinctively unfurled themselves and I handed over the cash.

Once I was through the turnstile, changes began bombarding me from every angle. There was no overpowering stench of piss because no one was pissing up the walls. Hundreds upon hundreds upon thousands upon millions upon hundreds of television cameras followed my every move. There were women and children in there, and black people as well. Big, large signs adorned every space on the wall that wasn't taken up by a TV camera, proclaiming 'No Atmosphere Allowed'.

As each change attacked me, it felt like a welt piercing my mind. Walking up the stairs to the terraces, I was struggling to hold it together. I grappled for the physical note I'd made, but it slipped from my grasp. I mentally reached for the mental note, but it fell out of my nose. I felt my head begin to spin again and knew that if I didn't act, and act fast, I would be in trouble, adrift in a world whose rules were unknown to me, a stranger in a strange land, a cunt.

'Fucking focus,' I said to myself, though one or two people nearby might have overheard.

I was nearly at the top of the stairs, the glare of the pitch was my light at the end of the tunnel. I stared into it, determined to reach it and carry out my plan. If I could just get to it and onto the terraces, I could fucking pile into any cunt who was there – West Ham, Chels, community liaison officer, who-fucking-ever – and create mayhem in their world, thus bringing a shred of normality back to mine.

Covering the sides of my eyes, I ploughed on, but with every step, I could feel my bottle slipping from my grasp. Me, the top top boy, a firm of my own. It was fucking beyond out of order because there was no fucking semblance of order. If anything, it was well out of chaos, but I'm not sure that works.

Somehow, I made it to the top of the stairs. Instantly, I felt my bottle flooding back. All those cunts had tried to sort me out, but they had fucking failed and now, now it was fucking payback time and a fucking half and some.

I pushed through the stewards in front of me, ready to run amok and wade into all and cunting sundry. But what I saw ripped my heart from my bodice, tore my very soul from wherever the fuck the soul is and delivered it the kicking-in of all fucking time: there were no fucking terraces.

Everything collapsed within me and I did the worst, most unimaginable thing of all: I ran.

epi=fucking=logue

This Saturday, Chelsea are playing Scunthorpe in the FA Cup. Scunthorpe are my second team for obvious reasons, though if you're thick as pigshit and twice as dense, it's because they have 'cunt' in their name. My eldest boy is currently using his blue WAP tooth fucking phone computer mobile thing to arrange for a virtual ruck to go off at the game. I don't really fucking understand it, but from what I can make out, they arrange a time and a place to meet in cyberspace, then take the information superhighway football special to get there and then kick shit out of each other by fucking tapping some fucking keys on a keypad. No broken bones. No black eyes. No stab wounds. No garrottings. The only thing that gets hurt is fucking pride. It's a fucking poof's game if you ask me, but when I start going on about it to Umberto, he just tells me to fuck off out of it by text message.

I didn't stop running that day for about three weeks. I suppose, in some fucking respects, I'm still running now, over ten years later. In that time, the changes that Dr Felchwarden Ph.D., MD, CUNT, TIT, FUCKWIT – he's retrained and now has even more fucking letters after his name – referred to have kept on coming. The game this Saturday is a fucking rarity in itself on account of it actually being on a Saturday and kicking off at three o'clock. That's a fucking collector's item these days, as rare as a Weetabix van (mint and boxed) in Dinky-toy terms. Nowadays, Chelsea could be playing on Monday, Tuesday, Wednesday, Thursday, Friday, Saturday, Sunday or Monday again. The kick-off could be at any fucking time from 11.00 in the morning to 10.38 at night. There's no First, Second, Third or Fourth divisions and there's a team called Rushden and fucking Diamonds in the fucking league. And that's just for fucking starters. I could go on, but it's a head-fucking-fuck.

For the first couple of years after that West Ham game, I roamed the country searching for football as I knew it. But everywhere I went the broom that was sweeping the game clean had already been before me. Sure, real, non-virtual violence at football persisted in some of the lower leagues, still does today in fact, and I found a few half-decent rucks to join in with. For a while, I was even a top boy in an Altrincham firm, but it was bollocks, a half-arsed attempt to keep a dying breed alive, to keep myself alive. I felt like a fucking Inca or Aztec except without the culture or architecture or hidden treasures.

I suppose I finally called it a day when they released that song about me in 1996, the one about 30 years of hurt. OK, so the cunts had got it wrong, it was nearer to 25 years of hurt, hurt that I'd inflicted on any cunt who came within 3 millinches of me (there's no fucking way I'm going metric, that's one change that can fuck right off to its Europhile fucking home), but they probably didn't do their homework, did they, or maybe 25 didn't scan or something. Anyway, the song fucking put it into per-fucking-spective for me; all that hurt that was down to me, all it had fucking done was provide some cunts with inspiration for a fucking song. What was the fucking point of that?

Yeah, I was low. Now I don't see it like that. Now I see it as the best fucking years of my life, especially as I'm currently a high-ranking civil servant living with my wife and two kids in North Harrow. It was an education as far as I'm concerned, and one that I came out of with a fucking masters degree, possibly even a Ph.D. But at that point in my life, I'd hit rock-lobster bottom, and all I kept hearing was that fucking song reminding me that everything I'd fought for, every cunt I'd kicked in, every slag I'd cut up, every mouthy muppet I'd seen to, all of it was just so that some cunts could fucking sing about it in a song.

To be honest, I still live in hope that it might one day all come back. That's why I've written this book. And because of the money as I said at the beginning. Just once more, I'd like to be stood in the middle of a swaying, baying mob of Chels as we tear into some cunts. I don't even care which cunts they are, though obviously if it was West Ham, Millwall, Arsenal, Tottenham or Manchester United, it would be that much better.

I still see some of the lads from time to time. One or two of them never got over that Sunday kick-off and live in a home for ex-football hooligans. It's not a bad place actually, set up by the Professional Ex-Hooligans Association and supported by charitable donations and the proceeds of various armed robberies. Others picked up the shreds of their lives and have made something of themselves: Gal is an arms dealer, Steve is Minister without Portfolio in the current Taiwanese administration and Gal is Sir Norman Foster. When we meet up, we have a laugh in the way other cunts mention children's programmes from their youth and piss themselves. But it's a hollow, empty, unfilled vacuum flask of a laugh. A laugh that says, yeah, we had joy, we had fun, we had Arsenal on the run, but the joy didn't last cause . . . cause fuck knows. Fuck knows why it didn't last. I mean, it wasn't as if we were doing any harm. Not really. We was just having a laugh, weren't we?

A few weeks ago, I went back to Stamford Bridge for the first time since that Braille fixture list-related fuck-up that led to the end of it all to see Chelsea playing Norwich. The Shed's gone now. And the North Bank. Even if Norwich had come down heavy-handed that day, there would have been nothing left for them to take; though to be fair, Norwich were always fucking pushovers and if they had come down heavy-handed thinking they could take the Shed, even the middle-class cunts in their middle-class trillion-pound execu-fucking-tive boxes could have run them.

I felt like an alien from an alien planet stepping into an alien land, but one that seemed as if I'd been there before, perhaps in another life. There was an unfamiliar familiarity to it as well as a familiar unfamiliarity.

Using a compass and my sense of smell, I managed to locate where the Shed had been and made my way over there. Using more precision instruments, a bigger compass, a protractor and a trombone, I found the exact centre of the Shed, the spot where I'd stood and kicked the absolute living shit out of more cunts than I care to remember in days gone by. Now all that was there was a red plastic seat. No blue plaque, no statue, no fucking fountain.

I crawled underneath the seat and, using a model replica of that burrowing vehicle from *Thunderbirds*, I began burrowing. It took a while, but eventually the hardness of the concrete gave way to a softness, a softness that made my heart leap for fucking joy. I continued burrowing, more carefully now, and soon I could see it, lying just where I had left it all those years ago: a testicle. I'd ripped it from the scrotal sac of some Scouse cunt in 1977 and buried it for some reason. At the time, I had no idea why – I'd eaten the other one – but it just seemed like the thing to do. Now I knew why I'd done it: so that I could dig it up all these years later.

Popping the surprisingly undecayed morsel into my mouth, I sat back in the seat, chewing and smiling at the same time (not fucking easy – try it).

'Excuse me, but I'm afraid you're sitting in my seat.'

I stopped chewing but continued smiling and looked up.

'Oh, I'm sorry,' I said. 'Here.'

I stood up and moved to one side.

'Thank you,' said the geezer.

'Not at all,' I said. And then I kicked the absolute living fuck out of the cunt.

The Fucking End